WOODWORK

Alfred Yarwood trained as a cabinet maker and then as a craft teacher before pursuing a career in education which included three posts as head of technical departments. He has written numerous articles for *Woodworker* and *Practical Woodworking* magazines, and is the author of more than a dozen textbooks for schools and colleges. He has a special interest in woodwork design, and is currently an examiner in Graphical Communication, Technical Drawing and Design and Craft.

D1341306

TEACH YOURSELF BOOKS

WOODWORK

A. Yarwood

TEACH YOURSELF BOOKS

Hodder and Stoughton

First published 1983

Copyright © 1983
A. Yarwood

British Library Cataloguing in Publication Data
Yarwood, A.
  Woodwork—(Teach yourself)
  1. Woodwork—Amateurs' manuals
  I. Title
  684'.08   TT185

ISBN 0 340 33775 3

Printed in Great Britain for
Hodder and Stoughton Educational,
a division of Hodder and Stoughton Ltd,
Mill Road, Dunton Green, Sevenoaks, Kent,
by Richard Clay (The Chaucer Press) Ltd,
Bungay, Suffolk.
Photoset by Rowland Phototypesetting Ltd,
Bury St Edmunds, Suffolk.

Contents

1

Wood

Introduction

Wood is a remarkable material. Its main value lies in the fact that if for every tree felled to produce timber, another tree were planted to replace it, there would always be sufficient timber for our needs. Wood is a material which is relatively easy to work to shape, yet is tough and strong. It possesses variations of beauty which other materials lack, is easily available from a large number of suppliers and is relatively cheap. It is one of the few constructional materials which can be worked at home without the need to purchase expensive machinery and with only a few tools.

Many hundreds of different species of trees are sawn into timbers, from which woodworkers make a vast range of articles. The timber-producing industry is international, with different types and qualities of timber coming from all parts of the world – building timbers from Canada, Russia and the Baltic, furniture timbers from Africa, South America, the USA and Japan, teak and ebony from Burma and India, Parana pine from Brazil and other special timbers from Australia. There is hardly a country in the world which does not engage in the trade.

There is also a world-wide trade in board materials manufactured mainly from wood. These include hardboards, plywoods, block-boards and chipboards, some of which can be purchased with one or both sides veneered with choice woods or with plastic sheets (laminates).

Hardwoods and softwoods

Woodworkers classify woods into two types – hardwoods and softwoods. *Hardwoods* are from trees with broad leaves – oak, ash, beech, mahogany and teak. *Softwoods* are from coniferous trees, such as larch, red deal (Scots pine) and spruce. Nearly all 'hardwoods' are harder than 'softwoods', but there are a few exceptions, such as balsa, which is very soft and very light in weight, but is a 'hardwood' to a woodworker because it is obtained from a broad-leaved tree. It grows in the tropical parts of the Americas and in Sri Lanka. Pitch pine on the other hand is a 'softwood', although it is very hard and difficult to work, because the pitch pine tree is coniferous.

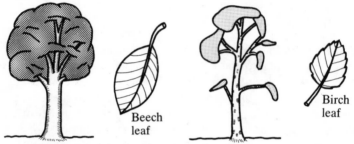

Fig. 1.1   'Broad-leaved' hardwood trees – beech and birch

Fig. 1.2   'Softwood' trees with needle shaped leaves – Scots pine and spruce

Botanically, the trees from which hardwoods are obtained are *Angiosperms* and the trees from which softwoods are obtained are *Gymnosperms*. Hardwoods are largely cellular in structure and softwoods are largely fibrous.

Processes of producing timber

The timber used for making articles from wood is the result of a series of processes. First, the tree from which the timber is obtained must be felled. Most of the tree felling throughout the world is now carried out with the aid of power saws, which are often chain saws. In poorer countries, or where the trees to be felled are growing in positions where the use of power saws is unsuitable, axes and hand crosscut saws are still used. When the tree has been felled, its branches and twigs are sawn or axed from the main trunk leaving a log (see Fig. 1.3). Sometimes the log will be sawn or axed to a square section known as a baulk (see Fig. 1.4) in the place where the tree was felled. The logs or baulks are transported to saw mills by animals (horses, mules, elephants etc.), by lorry, by train, by ship, or by being floated down rivers.

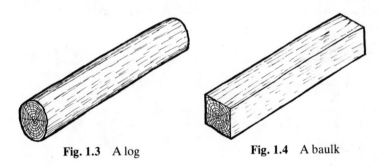

Fig. 1.3   A log

Fig. 1.4   A baulk

Shrinkage in green wood

Fig. 1.5 shows the cross-section of a log. The *bark* protects the living tree, the *cambium* is the growth layer of the tree; in most species an *annual ring* is laid down each year, all trees have *medullary rays*; (some cannot however be seen with the naked eye); the *heartwood* consists of dead cells and the *sapwood* carries liquids up the tree and consists of living cells.

A freshly felled tree contains a great deal of water. In some species as much as 50 per cent of the weight of 'green' wood can be water. 'Green' timber cannot be worked because tools will simply not cut such wood and it cannot be painted or polished because such 'finishes' peel off the wet surface. 'Green' wood also shrinks as it

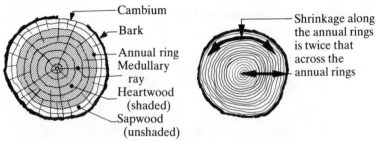

Fig. 1.5   End of a log   **Fig. 1.6**   Shrinkage

dries. The shrinkage along the direction of the annual rings is often twice as great as that across the rings (see Fig. 1.6). Because of this uneven shrinkage, as wood dries it can distort. Some examples of this distortion are given in Fig. 1.7. The drying, or seasoning, of wood must be carefully controlled if such distortion is to be avoided. 'Green' timber is heavier, but weaker than seasoned timber.

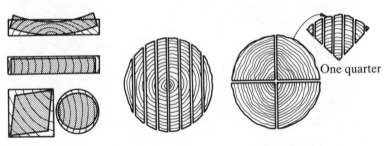

Fig. 1.7   Results of shrinkage   **Fig. 1.8**   Slash-sawn log   **Fig. 1.9**   Quarter-sawn log

Sawing of logs and baulks into boards

The logs are usually sawn into baulks before being sawn into planks and boards at the saw mill. Two principal methods of sawing logs and baulks into planks and boards are 'slash' sawing and 'quarter' sawing. Quarter-sawn boards are more expensive to produce than slash-sawn boards, but have the advantage of showing good quality 'figure' and of remaining flat and not 'warping' (see Figs 1.8 and 1.9). The resulting planks and boards must be dried or 'seasoned' before they are suitable for the making of wooden articles. Planks are 50 mm (2 in) or more thick; boards are less than 50 mm (2 in) thick.

Seasoning

Two methods of seasoning are commonly practised: *open-air* seasoning and *kiln* seasoning. Kilns are like giant ovens in which temperature and moisture are closely controlled to allow timber to be dried in six or seven weeks. Open-air seasoning is a longer process, taking up to a year or even longer. You may well have seen stacks of timber being seasoned and have noticed the careful orderly stacking, with 'piling sticks' to allow circulation of air.

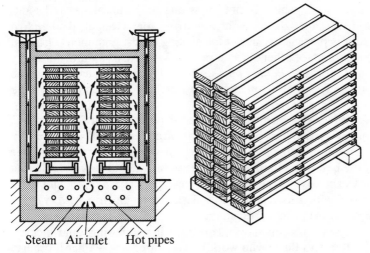

Steam Air inlet Hot pipes

Fig. 1.10 Kiln seasoning   **Fig. 1.11** Open-air seasoning

A wide variety of types of kiln for seasoning wood are constructed. Fig. 1.10 shows how one type functions. Sawn boards are stacked with piling sticks on to trolleys which are run into the kiln. Warm, humid air is circulated between the boards and extracts moisture from the wood as it moves between the boards. The cooled air drops to the outside of the stacks and is extracted via vents in the walls into the open air.

Fig. 1.11 shows a stack of sawn boards ready for open-air

seasoning. Such stacks are usually placed under the cover of a roof and are weighted on top with heavy boards. Note the piling sticks, exactly in line vertically above each other.

Woods available

A common building timber is *Scots pine*. It is never referred to by this name, but is called 'redwood' or 'red deal' or 'yellow deal'. It is a strong softwood and can be purchased in a range of qualities. The cheaper kinds are suitable for shed frames, building joists, fencing and so on. The better types are suitable for making good quality 'pine' furniture and fittings around the house. Other softwoods may be available, such as *spruce*, commonly called 'white deal' or 'whitewood', which is not so strong and durable as redwood. However, it is light in weight, and strong for its weight. *Western Red Cedar* is particularly useful for making sheds, greenhouse frames, fencing and for other outdoor purposes, where its natural durability is a great asset. *Parana pine*, a straight-grained, usually knot-free softwood, can also sometimes be purchased and comes from the monkey-puzzle tree.

Hardwoods which can usually be purchased are *African mahogany* – a rich pink brown; *ramin* – straight-grained and a uniform straw colour; *afrormosia* – deep brown with a good grain; *teak* – one of the best of all timbers, a rich deep brown and very durable, but very expensive. You may find you can purchase *oak* – a light straw colour, with a good grain and a 'flash' figure, and *ash* – a very tough wood with a pronounced grain.

Other woods you may find difficulty in purchasing, but which are of interest to those who work in wood are: *yew* – a hard, orange-brown softwood with a distinct decorative figure; *rosewood* – a handsome purple-brown hardwood with good grain markings; *ebony* – brown-black or black, a very hard wood for making 'treen'; *cherry* – even-grained, a pink-brown colour and *walnut* – a fine, well-figured hardwood used for furniture.

Purchasing wood

When you wish to buy wood, it is best to go to a timber yard if possible. There are several in most towns. Most of the people who run these yards will sell you either small or large quantities of wood and will often take great interest in what you are making. The second source of supply is 'do-it-yourself' shops, where small or large pieces of wood can easily be purchased. In some you can select for yourself the actual pieces you wish to buy. However these shops rarely carry as great a variety of timbers as timber yards.

Market forms

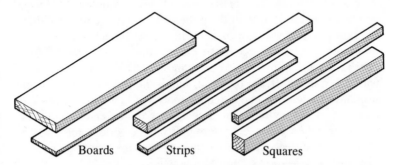

Fig. 1.12   Some common market forms

Boards planed both sides (PBS) can be purchased in thicknesses finishing 6 mm (¼ in), 10 mm (⅜ in), 13 mm (½ in), 16 mm (⅝ in), 19 mm (¾ in), 22 mm (⅞ in) or thicker. Such boards vary in width from about 150 mm (6 in) to as much as 300 mm (12 in). Strips of wood planed all round (PAR) of various sectional dimensions are often carried in stock sizes. Common sizes are: 45 mm by 22 mm (1¾ in × ⅞ in), 70 mm by 15 mm (2¾ in × ⅝ in) and 95 mm by 13 mm (3¾ in × ½ in). Common strip 'squares' are 22 mm (⅞ in) square, 35 mm (1⅜ in) square and 45 mm (1¾ in) square.

Unplaned wood is cheaper than wood which is ready planed. For some purposes, 'sawn' timber is quite suitable without needing to be planed smooth. If you are prepared to plane 'sawn' timber to the size you require, the resulting saving in cash may be worth while. Note that when intending to plane sawn timber, it is necessary to add about 6 mm (¼ in) to the width and 3 mm (⅛ in) to the thickness you need, to allow for the wood removed by planing. If you are attending classes, say in the evenings, at an educational establishment, the instructor will probably allow you to purchase timber from stores. Waste wood from demolished buildings or old fittings in houses may be another source of timber for those seeking a supply.

Faults and defects

As with everything else which you purchase, the quality of the wood you buy depends partly on the price you pay. If you wish to obtain the best possible value, look carefully at each piece you buy. You may find you can reject those pieces containing defects. When purchasing good quality timber at high prices, do not accept wood with any defects. If, on the other hand, the price is low, you may well have to accept some defective material. For some items made from wood, some types of defect do not matter a great deal. However, when you are attempting to make good quality objects from wood, defects can be a considerable nuisance and spoil the results. Fig. 1.13 shows some common defects.

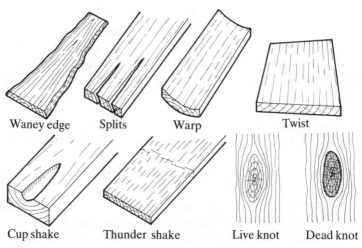

| Waney edge | Splits | Warp | Twist |

| Cup shake | Thunder shake | Live knot | Dead knot |

Fig. 1.13   Some common defects

Waney edge should lead to a lower price. The waney edge will have to be sawn off, which means some waste.

Splits are sometimes the result of bad seasoning practices.

Warps can be planed out if slight. However, if they are severe, the board can never be forced into a flat shape.

Twists are often the result of poor seasoning or bad storage. Twisted boards can sometimes be sawn and planed into narrow strips.

Cup shake is fairly common in cheaper softwoods.

Thunder shake only occurs in some tropical hardwoods. Boards with thunder shake will easily break across the shake.

Live knots may not be much trouble, as they are not liable to drop out.

Dead knots may drop out and leave a hole.

Manufactured boards

Manufactured board materials are often easier to purchase than 'solid' wood. They have the following advantages: they are of good quality, they do not shrink or expand when included in constructions, they can be purchased with a variety of face veneers and they can be obtained in large board sizes. A common standard board size is 2400 mm by 1200 mm (approximately 8 ft by 4 ft), although smaller sizes can also be purchased.

Plywoods

Plywoods are made from veneers, which are usually cut from logs on rotary cutting machines (see Fig. 1.14). Rotary cutting of veneers has the advantage that the veneers can be cut to any reasonable length, as the knife 'peels' the material from the log. Rotary cut veneers can lack grain and other figure beauty, however they are very suitable for the making of plywoods. Veneers for decorative purposes are more often cut on flat knife veneer cutting machines, in which a moving knife cuts off layer after layer of wood in thin slices (see Fig. 1.15). Plywoods are very strong relative to their thickness, because the boards are manufactured by gluing the plies together with the grain of alternate veneers running at right angles to each other (see Fig. 1.16). Plywoods are made from a large variety of different woods, in various thicknesses and in small or

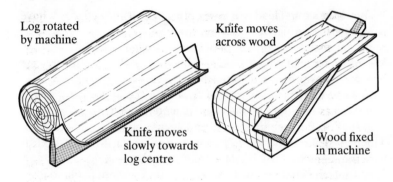

Fig. 1.14   Rotary cut veneer   **Fig. 1.15**   Flat knife-cut veneer

large boards. A common three-plywood thickness is 3 mm, but 2 mm or 4 mm three-ply boards are made. 6 mm five-ply, 9 mm seven-ply and other thicknesses are also obtainable. Plywoods can also be purchased faced on one or both sides with choice wood veneers, for example, mahogany, teak, afrormosia, oak or walnut, or with decorative plastic laminate sheets made from formaldehydes or from vinyls. They can also be purchased faced with aluminium or painted with special finishes.

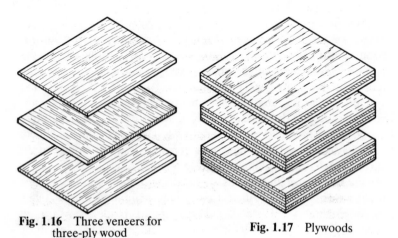

Fig. 1.16   Three veneers for three-ply wood   **Fig. 1.17**   Plywoods

The price of plywoods is determined by such factors as: the quality of the woods from which they are made, the adhesives employed for bonding the plies to each other and the form of decorative surface required. Some plywoods are made specifically for indoor work, when the adhesives gluing the plies together do not need to be resistant to water or weather. Others are made for external uses, such as building, for outside wall claddings and the making of boat hulls. Such external plywoods are usually classified as WBP – Water and Boil Proof – and are resistant to the most extreme conditions of weather and temperature. The bonding agents of such WBP plywoods are usually chemical resin adhesives, such as phenol formaldehyde.

Batten, block and lamin boards

Blockboards comprise a group of manufactured wood boards in which a 'core' of strips of wood is faced on both sides by veneers. The surface veneers are quite thick, from 1 to 3 mm (about $\frac{1}{16}$ to $\frac{1}{8}$ in) (see Fig. 1.18). Blockboards are manufactured from a large number of different woods and in a range of thicknesses, from 10 mm ($\frac{3}{8}$ in) up to 50 mm (2 in). The cheaper blockboards have cores formed from wide strips and are known as 'battenboards'. In 'blockboard' the cores consist of narrower strips. The highest quality, and hence most expensive, boards of this group, are the 'lamin' boards with very narrow core strips. The outer surface veneers of these boards are usually cut from better quality wood than the core material, although the best quality lamin boards are made from good quality wood throughout. Blockboards are very stable and flat, and can be purchased in boards of large surface area, the most common size being 2440 mm by 1220 mm (8 ft by 4 ft), but much larger boards can be purchased if required.

Hardboards

Hardboards (see Fig. 1.19) are made from pulped wood and are formed under heavy pressure and heat. They are inexpensive boards made in thicknesses usually of 2 mm and 3 mm, although 6 mm boards are also made. They can be obtained with a variety of surface finishes, such as polished, veneered or moulded. One useful form of hardboard is 'peg' board, in which holes are bored at regular intervals.

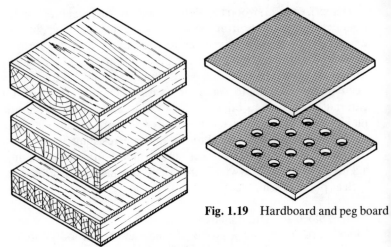

Fig. 1.19   Hardboard and peg board

Fig. 1.18   Batten, block and lamin boards

Chipboards

Chipboards are made from chips of wood, held together with a 'binder' – 90 per cent chips to 10 per cent binder. The binder is usually urea-formaldehyde, but in water-resistant chipboards, melamine formaldehyde or phenol formaldehyde would be employed. The chips vary in size and position within the boards, according to the purpose for which the boards are required. Of the three types shown in Fig. 1.20, three-layer chipboard is the one most frequently used by the general woodworker. Chipboard is an inexpensive material, relatively dense and heavy, and made in large boards of thicknesses from as little as 3 mm (⅛ in) up to 19 mm (¾ in). Boards with sanded, painted or veneered surfaces can be purchased.

Ready machined boards

A number of boards machined ready for use can be purchased (see Fig. 1.21). Among such boards are tongued and grooved floorboards, tongued and grooved match boarding and weatherboarding. Common flooring sizes are 100 mm by 22 mm (4 in by ⅞ in) and 140 mm by 22 mm (5½ in by ⅞ in) and common match boarding sizes are 100 mm by 16 mm (4 in by ⅝ in) and 100 mm by 10 mm (4 in by ⅜ in), although other sizes of these manufactured

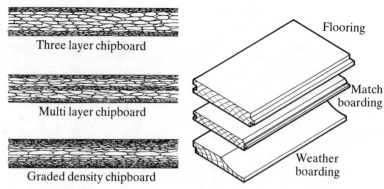

Three layer chipboard

Multi layer chipboard

Graded density chipboard

Fig. 1.20 Types of chipboard

Flooring

Match boarding

Weather boarding

Fig. 1.21 Some ready-machined timbers

boards are made. Match boarding is often used for cladding walls and ceilings. Weather boarding, sometimes obtainable, made from weather-resistant Western Red Cedar, is used principally as a cladding for walls, sheds, parts of greenhouses and other such buildings. Other ready machined wood materials include skirting boards, picture frame mouldings, quadrant mouldings and items such as dowels. Flooring, match boarding and skirting boards are commonly made from redwood. Mouldings and dowels are most commonly made from hardwoods, such as ramin and utile.

Plastic laminate sheet

A number of manufacturers produce a form of plastic laminate sheet made from papers impregnated with formaldehyde resins which are bonded together under pressure and heat. Some well known trade names of these sheets are 'Formica', 'Warerite', 'Armorboard', among others. These materials are of great interest to woodworkers. When veneered to hardboards, plywoods, block-boards or chipboards, they provide tough, hardwearing water and heat-resistant surfaces which are easy to clean and keep in good condition. The most common thickness of these plastic laminates is 1.5 mm (¹⁄₁₆ in), made up from three backing layers of tough kraft (brown) paper impregnated with phenol formaldehyde, a sheet of paper on which a decorative, often coloured, design is printed and a top sheet made from transparent cellulose paper impregnated with melamine formaldehyde (see Fig. 1.22). The group of papers is

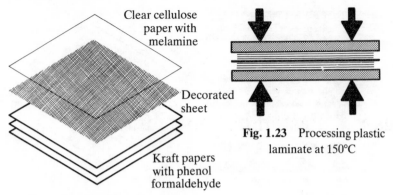

Clear cellulose
paper with
melamine

Decorated
sheet

Fig. 1.23   Processing plastic
laminate at 150°C

Kraft papers
with phenol
formaldehyde

Fig. 1.22   Sheets making up
plastic laminate

formed into a hard laminate by being pressed between polished
stainless steel plates at high pressure, and a temperature of approximately 150°C. The heat and pressure causes the formaldehyde
resins to set hard and permanently (see Fig. 1.23).

2

Fastenings and Fittings

During the past fifty years or so, an increasing number of people have become engaged in working with wood, either as work, as a hobby, or as a 'do-it-yourself' activity. Side by side with this increase, a number of new materials have been developed – chipboards, plastics, laminates and upholstery foams are just a few examples. A large do-it-yourself industry has also developed to supply the needs of the individual woodworker. Such developments have assisted the growth of a small industry which designs, manufactures and sells a very large range of fastenings and fittings for use with wood and its associated materials. These can be purchased from shops or mail-order firms specialising in supplying fastenings and fittings to either individuals or firms in small or large orders. As a result, when a woodworker requires any particular fastening or fitting, there is now a wide choice of different designs made from various materials in ranges of size.

A selection of a few of the most common of these fastenings and fittings is shown in this chapter. It is necessary to stress that only a small number from the large choice available are shown. An important group of fastenings – the 'knock-down' fittings – are not dealt with here, but will be described later in Chapter 6. The methods of fitting some of the fastenings (nails, screws, hinges and so on) are also dealt with in Chapter 6.

Nails

Most nails are made from carbon steel. Some are coated with zinc (galvanised) to protect against rusting. Hardboard pins are copper coated steel. Nails for boat making are made of copper. When nailing Western Red Cedar boards it is advisable to use nails made from aluminium. Fig. 2.1 shows the most common types of nails.

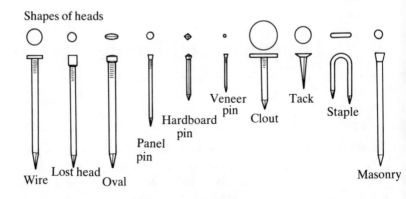

Fig. 2.1   Types of nails

Wire nails are the most common, measuring 25 mm to 150 mm (1 in to 6 in) in length. They are used for general carpentry such as floors, roofs and for fencing and packing-box making.

Lost head nails are a modern form of wire nail.

Oval nails are used for general fitting woodwork and furniture making. They range from 12 mm to 75 mm (½ in to 3 in) in length.

Panel pins are good light nails for general furniture work, measuring from 10 mm to 50 mm (⅜ in to 2 in) in length.

Hardboard pins are hardened nails, 20 mm (about ¾ in) long.

Veneer pins are very light nails, suitable for model making and vary from 10 mm to 25 mm (⅜ in to 1 in) in length.

Clouts are used for nailing fabrics and roofing felt to wood. They are often galvanised and sometimes copper, and measure from 12 mm to 50 mm (½ in to 2 in) long.

Tacks are mainly for upholstery work, measuring 12 mm and 15 mm (½ in and ⅝ in) long.

Staples are for nailing fabrics, for netting, etc, are made in various sizes and often galvanised.

Masonry nails are made from hardened steel and are usually 50 mm (2 in) long.

Wood screws

Wood screws are most often made from mild steel, but they are also made from other metals, such as brass, aluminium, bronze or stainless steel. Various coatings are added to some screws: zinc (galvanised), black lacquer (japanned), copper, brass, chromium and cadmium. Pozidriv screws are usually rust-proofed with coatings of zinc or cadmium. Coach bolts and screws are made from black mild steel.

Screws are available in a vast range of sizes. They are measured by length and diameter. The quoted lengths – from 5 mm up to 150 mm ($\frac{1}{4}$ in to 6 in) – are the effective length of the whole screw (see Fig. 2.2). Wood screw diameters are indicated by standard gauge sizes from 00 to 20 but larger diameters up to 50 gauge can be obtained. Gauge 00 is approximately 1 mm (about $\frac{1}{16}$ in); gauge 20 is marginally under 9 mm ($\frac{11}{32}$ in). The gauges which woodworkers use most frequently are 2, 4, 6, 8, 10 and 12.

Fig. 2.2 shows the most common types of screws and bolts.

Shapes of heads

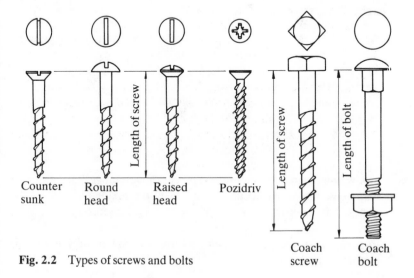

Fig. 2.2 Types of screws and bolts

Countersunk screws are general purpose screws. At least 75 per cent of all wood screws have countersunk heads.

Round head screws are really mis-named because the heads are not even half-round. These are for fixing thin metal fittings.

Raised head screws are used for screwing fittings such as locks and handles.

Pozidriv screws have twin-start threads for rapid 'driving' and are sometimes referred to as 'Pozidriv twinfast' screws.

Coach screws are for heavy constructional assembly work.

Coach bolts are also for heavy constructions. A spanner is necessary for tightening coach screws and coach bolts and their nuts.

In Fig 2.2 the shapes of the heads of each of the screws are shown along the upper edge of the illustration. The wood screws have screwdriver slots, either to take a straight screwdriver or to receive the tip of a Pozidriv screwdriver. The shanks of the coach bolts have squares under their heads to prevent the bolt from turning in the holes when nuts are tightened with spanners.

Some common screw hooks and screw eyes are illustrated in Fig. 2.3.

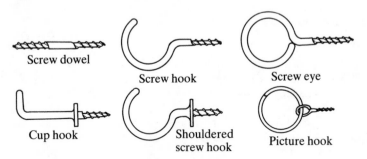

Fig. 2.3   Screw hooks and screw eyes

Screw dowels are for holding two pieces of wood together.

Cup hooks and screw hooks are mainly used for hanging small items in position. They can be steel, brass, or brass-plated.

Screw eyes have a variety of uses and are made of steel or brass.

Picture hooks are for hanging pictures and are usually made of copper-coated steel.

Other types of screws and screw fittings

Chipwood screws are used for screwing fittings such as hinges to chipboard. Usually galvanised, they are twin-start screws, like Pozidriv screws.

Self-tapping screws are made from hardened steel. Woodworkers find self-tapping screws of value when screwing wooden parts to sheet metal.

Mirror screws have a tapped hole into which a polished semi-spherical dome is fitted, to conceal the screw head.

Screw cups are brass or plated steel cups into which the head of countersunk screws can be fitted.

Plastic mirror cups are used for concealing the heads of countersunk screws.

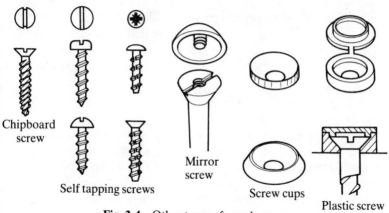

Chipboard
screw

Self tapping screws

Mirror
screw

Screw cups

Plastic screw
cup

Fig. 2.4   Other types of wood screws

Hinges

Sooner or later you will need to hang a door or hinge a box lid. Of the wide range of hinges which can be purchased today, eight are shown in Fig. 2.5. When hanging a door or hinging a box lid, a pair of hinges is usually necessary. For large doors such as wardrobe doors, three or even four hinges may be required. Choose the size of hinge most suitable for the work being undertaken. Hinges are fitted to woodwork with wood screws and made from a variety of materials; brass, steel and nylon are common. Platings of zinc, cadmium or paint are applied to some of the hinges available.

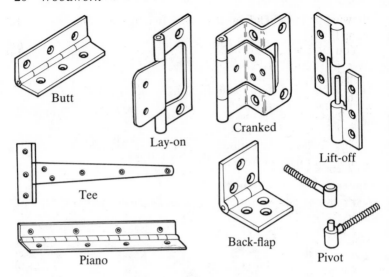

Fig. 2.5   Types of hinges

Butt hinges are a common form of door or box hinge. They need to be screwed into purpose-cut recesses in the work to which the hinges are fitted.

Lay-on hinges are usually made of zinc, cadmium or chromium-plated steel. They can be laid in position and screwed into place.

Cranked hinges are for hanging items such as casement windows.

Lift-off hinges enable the door to be lifted off if required.

Tee hinges are used for garden gates and shed doors.

Piano hinges are lightweight and used for various box lids.

Back flaps are for hinging flaps such as writing flaps or table flaps.

Pivot hinges are used for lightweight doors.

Catches, bolts and locks

When a door or lid has been hinged, it may be necessary to select some form of fitting by which it can be held in its closed position. The choice will be from catches, bolts or locks. Catches are made from metals or from plastic materials. They operate with the aid of ball bearings held by springs, by the action of magnetic strips or by purpose-shaped spring clips. Catches are made in a range of sizes to allow a choice depending on the size and weight of the door or lid being fitted.

You may decide to choose a bolt or a lock for holding a door you have just hung. Here again, a variety of types and sizes will be available. Bolts are usually fitted in position by being screwed to both the door and to its opening. Locks usually need to be screwed into purpose-cut recesses, which will need careful marking and accurate cutting if the lock is to function properly.

Fig. 2.6 shows a selection of the catches, bolts and locks available in shops or on order from mail catalogue firms.

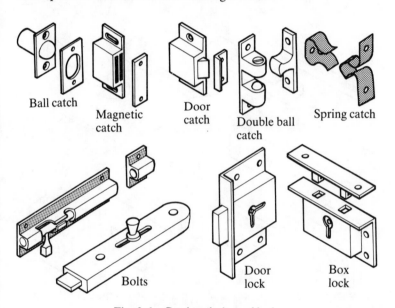

Fig. 2.6 Catches, bolts and locks

Handles

Drawer, door or box lid handles can be made by the woodworker to his own original designs from hardwoods such as beech, mahogany, teak. They can be turned on a lathe or formed with shaping tools at a bench. Hundreds, if not thousands, of different designs of handles are sold, which may be made from woods, metals or plastics. Purpose made wood handles – polished, painted or 'whitewood' –

may be turned or machined. Metal handles from brass, steel or aluminium can be obtained. These may be polished, finished matt, plated with chromium, brass or bronze and may be sold with a gold, silver or bronze finish. If made from aluminium, they may be finished by being anodised in a variety of colours. Handles made of plastic materials are also available.

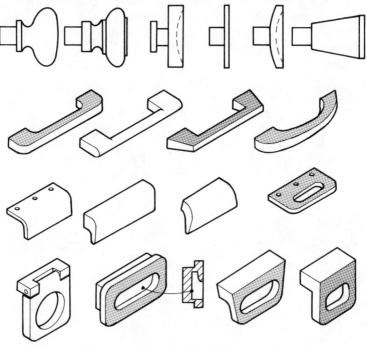

Fig. 2.7   Handles

A number of different handle forms are shown in Fig. 2.7. These are only a very small selection of those available either from shops or by mail order from catalogues. Some of the handles show shapes suitable for making by a woodworker himself.

Wall fittings and wall plugs

Wall plates and wall plugs are designed to help secure fittings and items of woodwork you have made to walls. Mirror plates or other forms of wall plate can be screwed to the back of the article made from wood. Wall plugs are then inserted into holes bored in the wall with appropriate sizes of wall masonry drills. The article is then screwed to the wall with screws through the wall plate into the wall plug. Two wall plates and four types of wall plug are shown in Fig. 2.8.

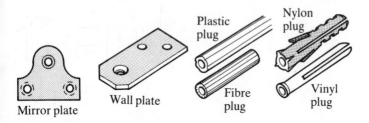

Fig. 2.8   Wall plates and plugs

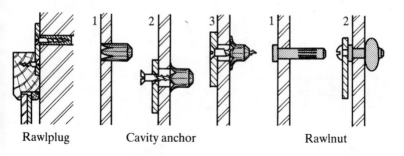

Fig. 2.9   Wall plugs

A framed mirror is shown fixed to a wall by this method in Fig. 2.9. The other drawings of this illustration show stages in the fitting of two special types of wall plugs designed for fixing articles to walls made from building boards. Cavity anchor plugs and 'Rawlnuts' are made from materials which are flexible and which expand against the rear of the wall as the screw (or bolt) of the plug is driven tightly home. Rawlnuts are fitted with a nut and bolt, whereas cavity plugs are expanded under the action of driving a wood screw into the plug.

Mirror clips, sliding door fittings and shelf support clips

Mirror clips are used for fastening mirrors to backings of lamin board, plywood or chipboard and usually brass plated.

Sliding door fittings are for small glass or manufactured board doors. That shown in Fig. 2.10 is one of the most simple. Larger doors require some form of roller fitting.

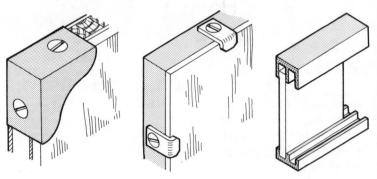

Fig. 2.10   Mirror clips and a sliding door fitting

Shelf supports Four different types of shelf support are shown in Fig. 2.11. One part of the fitting is screwed to the inside face of, say, a bookrack side, or is fitted into holes in the side. The second part fits into the first and supports the shelf. These fittings are designed to allow a variety of spacings between shelves.

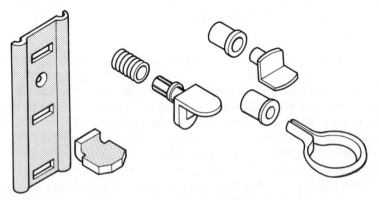

Fig. 2.11   Shelf support fittings

3

Hand Tools

Hand tools can be expensive, so some words of advice about purchasing them may well be useful. Always buy the best you can afford at the time of purchase. Well-made hand tools, given regular maintenance, will give good, constant service for many years and will often last a lifetime. Before buying any tool, look around the shops and through catalogues to see what is available. Compare designs and costs. Handle the tool. Does it feel well balanced? Is it comfortable to hold and handle? Is it made by a firm of good repute? Is it exactly what you are looking for? If you add to your tool kit as the need arises, the resulting kit will be better suited to your needs than if it is purchased all at once. Knowledge about tools comes from handling and using them, and part of that knowledge is gained from the experience of buying them.

Saws

There are not many woodworking projects which can be attempted without using saws at some stage. Four types will be described here. Three of these are for cutting along straight lines – handsaws and two 'backed' saws. The fourth is for cutting along curved lines – the coping saw. The two saws with backs are the tenon saw and the dovetail saw.

Handsaws
Handsaws are generally available with blade lengths from 500 mm (20 in) up to 650 mm (26 in), in 50 mm (2 in) steps. There are two

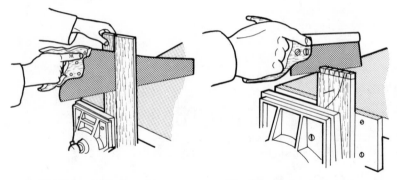

Fig. 3.1 A handsaw in use   **Fig. 3.2** A dovetail saw in use

main types of handsaws; those with crosscut teeth and those with rip teeth. Nowadays handsaws of any size tend to be found with crosscut teeth, but the teeth can be altered when they are sharpened if a rip saw is wanted. The two names, crosscut and rip, are self-explanatory, as the teeth are designed for cutting across the grain or for 'ripping' down the grain. The number of 'teeth per inch' (TPI) may vary from 10 TPI in the case of a crosscut saw, to as few as 4 TPI in rip saws. Many handsaws have a number stamped on the blade near to the handle giving the number of TPI of the saw. Handsaws with 500 mm (20 in) blades are often called 'panel' saws. They were traditionally used for sawing panelling to size. Generally speaking, two handsaws, one with a 600 mm (24 in) blade and 6 TPI sharpened with rip teeth, the other with a 500 mm (20 in) blade and 10 TPI crosscut teeth, will cover any work requiring the use of a handsaw.

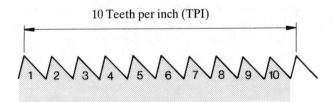

Fig. 3.3   Teeth per inch

Sharpening handsaws

The sharpening of the teeth of saws requires a fair degree of skill, which can only be gained with practice. The teeth of wood saws should be sharpened in three stages. The correct tool for carrying out the sharpening is a saw file. The drawings of Fig. 3.6 show the stages. First, the teeth should be 'topped' by filing with a flat file run along the teeth edges to ensure they are all level. Secondly, the teeth should be re-sharpened – whether they are crosscut or rip – with a triangular saw file. Crosscut teeth are filed so that alternate teeth are sharpened at an angle of 60°, so forming small, knife-like cutting edges along the length of the saw. Rip teeth are filed at 90° to the blade, which produces a series of plane-like cutting edges. Third, the saw should be 'set' so that the teeth are in turn bent outwards, each in an opposite direction to the one each side. This 'setting' results in a saw cut which is wider at the cutting edge than is the thickness of the saw blade. This effectively prevents a saw from binding in its own cut or 'kerf'. Saw setting can be carried out using purpose-made saw-setting pliers.

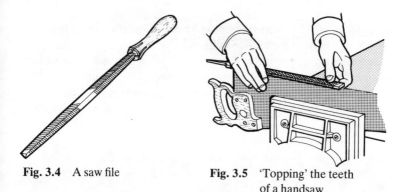

Fig. 3.4 A saw file

Fig. 3.5 'Topping' the teeth of a handsaw

Two other types of wood saw teeth are shown in Fig. 3.7. These are 'fleam' teeth and 'gulleted fleam' teeth. In both these types the saw cuts on both forward and return strokes. Gulleted fleam teeth are designed for cutting 'green' timber, as when sawing branches from living or fallen trees.

Ideally saws should be maintained free from rust. This is best achieved by hanging them in racks in a reasonably dry room or in a

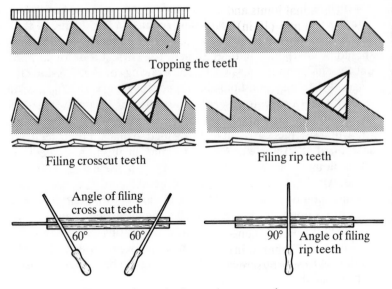

Fig. 3.6   Stages in sharpening saw teeth

workshop. If they must be kept in an area which tends to become damp, store them with some bags of moisture-absorbing silica gel. Many experienced workers carry a small piece of candle in a pocket of their working clothes. If this is rubbed occasionally along the sides of a wood saw blade, it acts as a good lubricant which allows the saw to run freely in its kerf without staining the wood being sawn.

Fig. 3.7   Fleam saw teeth and gulleted saw teeth

Backsaws

Backsaws are made with blades of thin gauge steel with a brass (sometimes steel) stiffening back fitted along the top of the blade. The function of this back is to prevent the blade buckling under working pressure. Backsaws are designed for sawing the parts of constructional joints and are usually made in three sizes – 200 mm (8 in), 250 mm (10 in) and 300 mm (12 in). The 200 mm type is normally referred to as a dovetail saw and the two larger types as tenon saws. Larger (350 mm) tenon saws will also be found. Dovetail saws have as many as 20 teeth to the inch and tenon saws between 12 and 15 TPI. Dovetail saws are for accurate sawing of light work. A pair of backsaws – a 200 mm dovetail and a 300 mm tenon – will cover practically all the work required of this kind of saw.

Coping saws
A coping saw consists of a spring steel frame into which disposable thin blades are fitted between pins in the frame. The blades are thrown away when they break or when their teeth become worn. Coping saws are designed for cutting along curved lines. The blades are about 150 mm (6 in) long. The steel frame is tensioned to hold the blade firmly by screwing the handle into its holding bolt after the blade has been fitted. Both the handle and its bolt and the pin holding the blade at the other end of the frame, can be rotated through 360°, to allow the blade to be worked at any angle to the frame.

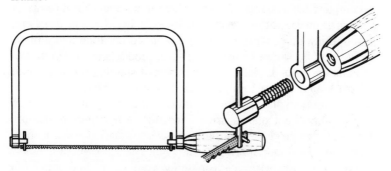

Fig. 3.8   A coping saw

Other saws for shaped work
Other saws for cutting along curved lines in wood will occasionally be found in tool kits. Bowsaws with wooden frames, in which a blade is tensioned by twisted twine between the frame parts, were at one time in very common use. Narrow-bladed keyhole saws and compass saws will also sometimes be found. These three saws are

not as commonly used now as in the past. The work they were designed for is now largely carried out with hand-held power tools. Fretsaws are another type of saw, used for sawing intricate curved lines in thin wood. Fretsaws consist of thin spring steel blades held in a spring steel frame.

Planes

Woodworking planes are designed for forming wood to finished sizes and shapes and to obtain a smooth surface finish as they do so. There is a large variety of planes from which to choose as the different types are designed to cater for the variety of circumstances which can be encountered when working in wood. Modern woodwork planes are mostly made of metal, with handles of wood. All parts of modern planes are replaceable, so that should a part become broken or worn out it can be replaced at minimal cost. The cutting blades of modern planes are adjustable for depth of cut, the adjustment being under finger control either by knurled nuts or levers.

Bench planes

A complete set of bench planes is three in number, all of the same pattern as the smoothing plane illustrated in Fig. 3.9. The three are: a smoothing plane with a body 245 mm (9¾ in) long and a blade (plane 'iron') 50 mm (2 in) wide, a jack plane, either 255 mm or 380 mm (14 in or 15 in) long and with a 50 mm or 60 mm (2 in or 2⅜ in) blade, and a jointer plane 560 mm or 610 mm (22 in or 24 in) long, with blades either 60 mm or 70 mm (2⅜ in or 2⅝ in) in width. Smoothing planes are by far the most common and are designed for producing a flat, smooth surface ready for final smoothing by sandpapering. Jack planes are for general heavy planing of woodwork, such as planing wood to finished sizes from sawn material or for planing away the bulk of material when forming parts to shape. Jointer planes are basically for 'shooting' or planing edges of boards quite straight, ready for edge jointing boards to one another. Because edge jointing is not so common nowadays, due to the increasing use of manufactured boards, jointer planes are not so widely used as in the past.

The bodies of this group of bench planes are made from good

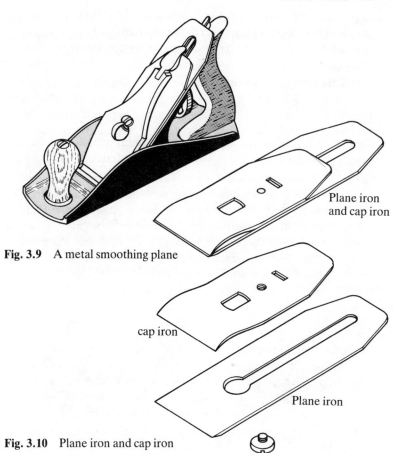

Fig. 3.9 A metal smoothing plane

Plane iron
and cap iron

cap iron

Plane iron

Fig. 3.10 Plane iron and cap iron

quality, fine cast iron. This is a brittle material, so must be treated with some care. If a plane were to be dropped on to a concrete workshop floor, there would be a strong possibility that the plane body would break at its weakest point; i.e. across the mouth of the plane. Adjustments of the depth of cut and the lateral position of the cutting blade are effected with the aid of a knurled adjusting knob and a lateral adjusting lever. These are placed just in front of the plane handle where they are under the immediate control of the thumb and forefinger. The width of the mouth opening through which shavings are ejected can be set by moving the frog of the plane with the aid of the frog-adjusting screws, seen when the plane blade is removed from the body. The bases of all metal planes are ground flat, straight and square. They remain flat even after many years of continuous use.

All planes will only work effectively and efficiently if the edges of the cutting blades are kept sharp. To sharpen the blade of a bench plane remove the plane 'iron' with its cap iron from the plane body by lifting and withdrawing the lever cap. Then remove the cap iron from the blade with a screwdriver. The edge of the lever cap can be used in lieu of a screwdriver. Spread thin lubricating oil over the surface of a medium grade oilstone. Holding the blade at an angle of 30° to the surface of the stone, work the blade over its surface until a 'burr' is raised on the back of the blade. Be careful to ensure that the whole surface of the oilstone is used as far as is possible, to avoid uneven wearing of the stone's surface. To ensure that the blade is sharpened at the correct angle, a honing-guide can be used as shown in Fig. 3.11. When a 'burr' has been raised, turn over the blade and,

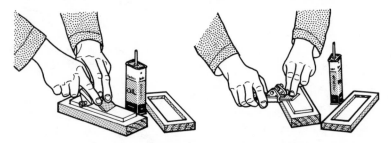

Fig. 3.11 Stages in sharpening a plane blade

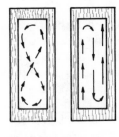

Fig. 3.12 Cover the whole surface of an oilstone

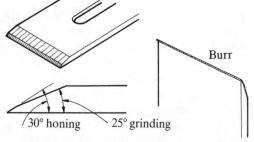

Fig. 3.13 Grinding and honing angles and a sharpening 'burr'

30° honing   25° grinding

Burr

holding it perfectly flat on the oilstone, work the blade over the stone to remove the burr. To remove the burr completely, the sequence of operations should be repeated several times. This weakens the burr, which can be finally removed by pushing the sharpened end into a piece of waste softwood.

Depending on the kind of wood being planed, the cap iron can be set to as little as 1 mm (¹⁄₃₂ in approximately) from the cutting edge (when hard, cross-grained wood is being worked). When planing straight-grained softwoods, the setting can be as much as 1.5 mm (¹⁄₁₆ in). After setting the position of the cap iron and screwing it back on the blade, the two are then replaced in the body and fixed in place by depressing the lever of the lever cap. The cut can then be adjusted with the aid of the setting knob and lever. A smear of candle grease over the base of a plane will assist in the smooth running of the plane over wood as it is removing shavings.

Block plane

For obtaining an ultra-smooth finish, a well sharpened block plane (see Fig. 3.14) will prove to be an invaluable tool. This plane does not possess a cap iron, but the blade is set at a very low angle of 20° to the base and is upside-down compared to the blade position of bench planes. These planes are quite short, being a mere 150 mm or 180 mm (6 in or 7 in) long, with cutters only 40 mm (1⅝ in) wide. They are thus fairly easy to control and apart from their primary function of obtaining a very smooth surface finish, they are a good plane for the type of work where one is compelled to work one-handed. This is because a block plane is designed to fit snugly into the palm of one's hand.

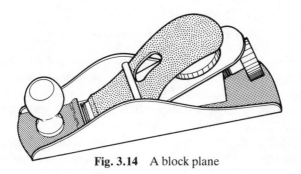

Fig. 3.14 A block plane

Other planes

Five planes for more specialised shaping of wood are: the rebate plane, the shoulder plane, the plough plane, combination planes, and the router plane. In the rebate and shoulder planes the blade extends through each side of the body. These planes can thus be used for cutting rebates (see Fig. 3.15). In the rebate plane, the blade can usually be fitted either centrally along the body (for normal rebate cutting) or at the front of the body, in a 'bull nose' position (for cutting stopped rebates). A fence and a depth stop are also fitted to a rebate plane to guide the plane accurately while working the width and depth of a rebate. The shoulder plane, with a 20° low angle, upside-down cutter is designed for very fine and accurate rebating, or, as its name implies, for trueing the shoulders of features such as tenons (shown in Fig. 3.16).

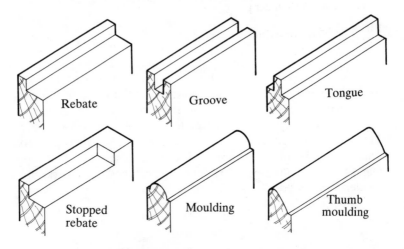

Fig. 3.15   Terms for shaped edges

Plough planes (an exploded drawing of one is given in Fig. 3.17) are designed mainly for planing grooves. A standard plough plane will take a range of cutters from 3 mm to 13 mm (⅛ in to ½ in). Again a guiding fence and depth stop are fitted to plough planes. The guide fence can be fitted to either side of the plane body.

A plane developed from the plough plane is the so-called 'combination' plane, designed not only to cut grooves, but also to plane

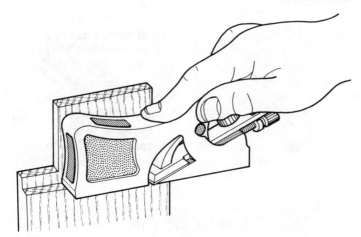

Fig. 3.16 A shoulder plane trimming the shoulder of a tenon

mouldings. The drawings of Fig. 3.18 show a combination plane working a groove and a small moulding. Fig. 3.19 shows a typical range of cutters for this particular plane.

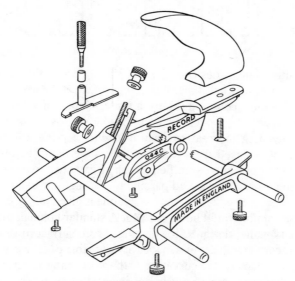

Fig. 3.17 An exploded drawing of a plough plane
(drawing by courtesy of Bahco Record Tools)

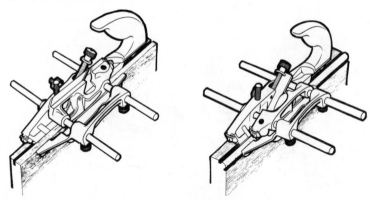

Fig. 3.18   Grooving and moulding with a combination plane
(drawings by courtesy of Bahco Record Tools)

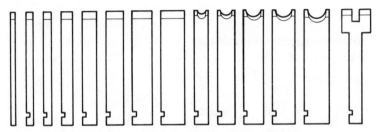

Fig. 3.19   A range of cutters for a combination plane

The router plane is designed for any planing where the blade of the tool is working at a distance below the surface of the wood being worked. The most common use for a router plane is in cutting the bottom surfaces of grooves for housing joints. This plane is also ideal for levelling the rear surface of a relief carving where the carved detail is raised from a flat surface some depth below the surface of the wood surround. Fences can be fixed to a router plane to allow the tool to be worked parallel to a straight or to a curved edge.

A plane not illustrated here, but which you may come across, is the compass plane, designed for planing curved surfaces, whether concave or convex. This tool is made with a flexible steel base which can be adjusted to suit the curvature of the work being undertaken. This adjustment is carried out by means of a screw worked by a milled nut. When using this plane the direction of the grain of the

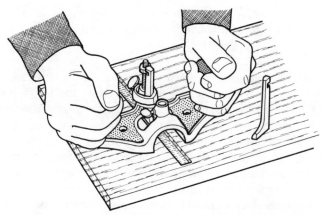

Fig. 3.20 A router plane clearing the bottom of a housing groove

wood must be noted so the plane can be used in the correct direction to avoid tearing or splintering the surfaces being worked.

Chisels and gouges

Chisels and gouges are an important group of woodworking tools. These are the tools with which the more intricate shaping of timber is carried out. Chisels differ basically from gouges in that they are essentially flat across their working faces, whereas gouges are made with blades which are curved in section. Both chisels and gouges are

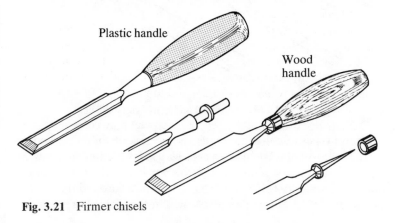

Plastic handle

Wood handle

Fig. 3.21 Firmer chisels

made in a large variety of different types and sizes, with a number of different forms of handles made from different materials.

Chisels

The common bench chisel is known as a 'firmer' chisel. This name is possibly derived from 'former'; a name denoting the forming of wood for which this type of chisel is largely used. Firmer chisels are made either bevel-edged or with blades of rectangular section. A set of five chisels of 3 mm, 6 mm, 13 mm, 19 mm and 25 mm (⅛ in, ¼ in, ½ in, ¾ in and 1 in) width should be sufficient to meet most of your needs. Other sizes can however be purchased, and two in particular – 1.5 mm (¹⁄₁₆ in) and 38 mm (1½ in) – may prove to be of value for some forms of work. Bevel-edged firmer chisels have the advantage of being able to be worked into angled corners, when cutting dovetail joints, for example. The handles of firmer chisels are made from a tough plastic called cellulose acetate butyrate (CAB) or from two different woods, ash or box. The modern plastic handle is virtually unbreakable, even being able to withstand hammer blows without fracture, but they can tend to be somewhat uncomfortable when used under hand pressure.

Fig. 3.22   Mortise chisel and heavy-duty chisel

Several types of chisel are made for the task of chopping wood, i.e. the removal of waste when a chisel is used in conjunction with a mallet or a hammer. These include the box-handled mortise chisel and the heavy-duty chisel which has a steel band around the top of the handle. Both of these are illustrated in Fig. 3.22. If a mallet is used on the heavy-duty chisel, the mallet head is quickly damaged under the action of the steel ring, so use a hammer with this chisel. A wide paring chisel (see Fig. 3.30) is a useful addition to a tool kit. This chisel with its long blade must not be used with a mallet. It is designed for paring under hand pressure and is made in a variety of sizes, but a single wide paring chisel, say of 30 mm (1¼ in) width, can be a useful addition to the woodworker's tool kit.

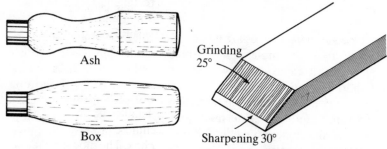

Fig. 3.23   Chisel handles

Fig. 3.24   Grinding and sharpening angles for chisels

The method of sharpening chisels is identical to that of sharpening plane blades, which was described on page 32. It is perhaps preferable to sharpen mortise chisels, and other chisels which are to be used for chopping, with the honing angle at 35° rather than at 30°. This increase in angle makes for a stronger cutting edge which is less liable to fracture under the force of mallet blows. Sharpened chisels should be stored in a wooden box or hung in purpose-made racks so that the sharp edges are covered as a safety precaution.

Gouges

Two types of bench gouge are made. These are known as firmer gouges with the sharpening bevel on the outside of the curve of the blade, and scribing gouges with the sharpening bevel on the inside of the curve. Firmer gouges are designed for the heavy work of cutting wood to shape, such as in heavy carved work, but are equally useful in the shaping of rounded recesses. Scribing gouges were originally designed for the shaping of 'scribed' tenon shoulders in frames made with rails with moulded edges. Scribing gouges still have their uses in modern work. Both firmer and scribing gouges are made in a variety of blade widths of different curvatures.

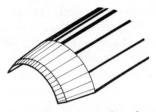

Fig. 3.25 Cutting edge of a firmer gouge

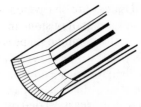

Fig. 3.26 Cutting edge of a scribing gouge

Woodcarving gouges are lighter in weight than bench gouges and made in an enormous range of blade widths and blade sectional shapes. An experienced woodcarver could well possess several hundred carving gouges of different sizes and shapes. Carving tools are generally sharpened in a manner which is somewhat different from that used for bench chisels and gouges. They are best sharpened with a double bevel of 25° on one side and 5° on the other, rather than 30° on one side and flat on the other (as would be the case for bench chisels and gouges).

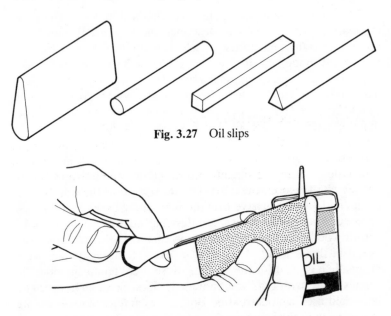

Fig. 3.27 Oil slips

Fig. 3.28 Sharpening a gouge

Gouges are sharpened with the aid of oilstone slips. These are small pieces of oilstone made in a variety of shapes (see Fig. 3.27). The most common shape is the left-hand one of the four in Fig. 3.27. The curved part of an oilslip is used for honing inside the curved part of the cutting edge of the gouge and the outer part of the curve is sharpened on a flat oilstone. In all other respects, sharpening of bench gouges is carried out as for chisels and for plane blades.

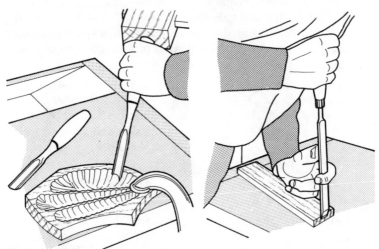

Fig. 3.29 Using a carving gouge   **Fig. 3.30** A paring chisel

Measuring and marking tools

No matter what the size of the work being undertaken, an essential feature of working in wood is to ensure that each part is made accurately to size and, equally important, is 'square'. Nothing looks worse to the woodworker than work made out-of-shape because size and squareness have been neglected. Rules, marking knives, squares and gauges assist in achieving accuracy of size and in ensuring that the finished work is square.

Rules

The choice of rule will be between a wood or nylon four-fold or two-fold rule, a steel rule or a measuring tape. Measuring tapes have much in their favour. Rule tapes are made with flexible steel blades, coated with a tough plastic finish which will resist wear, tarnishing or corrosion. The tapes are rolled within their own steel or plastic cases. They are graduated in metric units (centimetres and millimetres), and usually also in imperial units (feet and inches). A number of different tapes are on sale. One measuring up to 3 m (9 ft plus) on a 13 mm (½ in) wide tape would be suitable for nearly all purposes. Such a tape is illustrated in Fig. 3.31. Tape rules of this type can be used in the same way as can the more traditional nylon, wood or steel rules, and have the advantages that they are virtually unbreakable, can be stored in a small space and can measure longer lengths than the more traditional types of 12 in (30 cm) and 24 in (60 cm) rules.

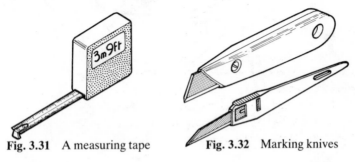

Fig. 3.31   A measuring tape   **Fig. 3.32**   Marking knives

Knives
Marking knives for cutting thin material or for marking lines which are to be cut by saws or other tools are made in a variety of sizes and shapes. Typical examples are shown in Fig. 3.32. The lower of those illustrated is a cheap 'throw away' knife, but with regular sharpening these can be made to last a considerable time. The upper knife has a blade which is held in a containing handle, in which several spare blades are carried.

Squares
Right from the start of making any piece of work from wood, it is essential that the parts are sawn square, planed square, and that when it has been constructed, its parts fit together so that the completed job is square. When work is glued together, it must again be tested for squareness before the glue sets hard. This repeated necessity for ensuring that the angle of 90° is observed throughout,

emphasises the importance of try squares, which are an essential item in any woodworker's tool kit. Try squares of differing blade lengths are available. Possibly the one most frequently employed is one with a 230 mm (9 in) blade, but occasionally one with a 310 mm (12 in) blade will be of value. A smaller 152 mm (6 in) bladed square is also useful on occasions.

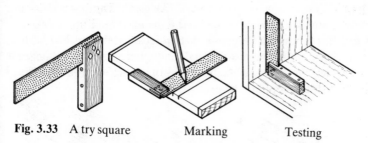

Fig. 3.33   A try square   Marking   Testing

If the blade of a try square becomes out-of-square for any reason, the tool becomes rather useless. Thus this tool should be treated with some care, not allowed to be dropped, and stored in purpose-made racks or boxes. To check the accuracy of a try square, use the method shown in Fig. 3.34. If inaccuracies are discovered, the blade can be carefully filed to exact squareness again.

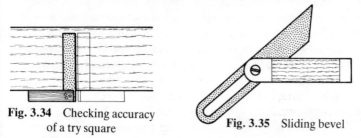

Fig. 3.34   Checking accuracy
of a try square   **Fig. 3.35**   Sliding bevel

Sliding bevels, which can be set to any desired angle, are similar to try squares in that they are used for marking and testing angles. Instead of being permanently set to 90°, like try squares, the angle of the blade of a bevel to its stock can be varied.

Gauges

Gauges are designed for marking lines parallel to edges and faces of pieces of wood. Three kinds of gauge are available. These are the marking gauge with a marking point made from hardened steel, the cutting gauge, in which the steel point is replaced by a small knife, and the mortise gauge in which two hardened steel spurs, adjustable for width, will mark a pair of parallel lines suitable for the marking out of mortises and tenons. Marking gauges are used when marking the widths and thicknesses of wood before planing and for marking lines of constructional joints with the grain. Cutting gauges are more useful when marking across the grain, where a marking gauge would not produce a clean line. When setting the spurs of a mortise gauge for marking out mortise and tenon joints, the usual practice is to set the twin spurs of the gauge to the exact width of the chisel employed for chopping the mortise.

Fig. 3.36   Marking, cutting and mortise gauges

Marking and cutting gauges are usually made of beech. The best gauges have brass inserts set into their stocks to resist the wear that the face will receive by constant use. Mortise gauge stocks and handles are often made from rosewood and other parts are made from brass. The marking spurs and cutting knives of all gauges are made from steel.

Hammers and mallets

Three hammers are of interest to woodworkers: pin hammers with 100 gram (3½ oz) heads; Warrington pattern hammers with 180 gram to 620 gram (6 oz to 20 oz) heads, of which a 350 gram (12 oz) head is possibly the most common, and claw hammers, generally with 620 gram (20 oz) heads. Pin hammers are suitable for light work and for model making; the Warrington pattern hammer is suitable for general purpose woodwork. The claw hammer is a heavy carpentry tool and has the advantage of a claw with which nails can be removed.

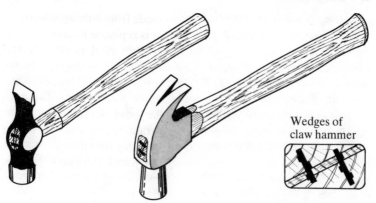

Fig. 3.37 Warrington pattern and claw hammers

Hammer heads are made from cast steel. Their working ends are known as 'peins'. Pin and Warrington pattern hammers have round and cross peins. The handles, or shafts, of these tools are usually made from best quality hickory – a hard, tough, springy wood from America. Some modern hammer shafts are made from tubular steel and fibre glass. Heads are secured to the shafts with steel wedges crossing wooden wedges or, in the case of non-wooden handles, the head is bonded within the eye of the hammer head with epoxy resin.

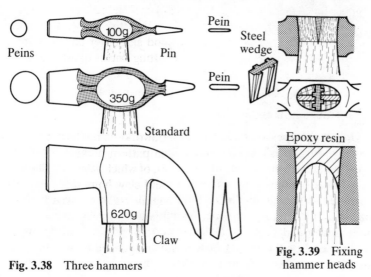

Fig. 3.38 Three hammers

Fig. 3.39 Fixing hammer heads

In the design of hammers, handle lengths are made so as to be suitable for giving an efficient delivery of a blow by the head. When using hammers, take advantage of this and do not 'strangle the hammer'. Use the full length of the handle. About the only maintenance which hammers will require is to ensure that the peins are clean and free of dirt, grease, hard glue and so on. The surfaces of the peins can be cleaned on fine sandpaper. Regular attention to the tightness of heads on handles is also desirable.

A set of nail punches is a useful addition to a tool kit. Punches like those illustrated in Fig. 3.41 can be purchased in different sizes, suitable for use with as fine a nail as a veneer pin up to the heavier wire nails.

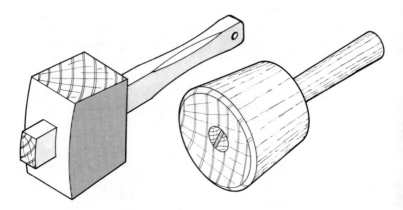

Fig. 3.40 Carpenter's and carving mallets

Only two types of mallet need be considered. These are the so-called carpenter's mallet and the carver's mallet. These tools are usually made from beech, and sizes of 125 mm (5 in) or 150 mm (6 in) head lengths for a carpenter's mallet are suitable for most purposes. A carver's mallet of 150 mm (6 in) diameter is a suitable size. Carver's mallets can be loaded with lead, which has been melted into and hammered tightly into holes bored in the upper circular end of the mallet head. The extra weight this produces allows an easy swing of the tool when in use.

Pincers

Pincers are designed for taking out nails. When choosing a pair of pincers, it is advisable to purchase as large a pair as is available, following the principle that the longer the handles of this tool, the greater the leverage they will exert and the larger the size of nail which can be extracted. Always protect work with a flat piece of waste wood against the quite severe bruising which a pair of pincers can cause.

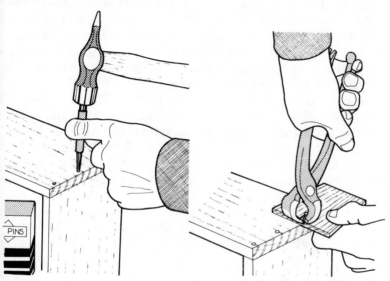

Fig. 3.41 Punching a nail head below the wood surface

Fig. 3.42 Removing a nail with pincers

Screwdrivers

Screwdrivers are manufactured in all shapes, sizes and colours. With the advent of Pozidriv screws, screwdrivers with Pozidriv tips are almost as common as the more traditional type, with a tip for fitting into screwed slots. Three sizes of Pozidriv screwdrivers are commonly available with tip sizes 1, 2 and 3 and although wood-workers will have little need for the largest (size 3), it is advisable to carry that size in your tool kit. Apart from selecting the appropriate blade to suit the screw head, lengths of handles and blades are of importance. Longer handles tend to provide greater leverage when inserting or removing screws, yet short, stubby screwdrivers can be of value when working in areas where space is restricted. Plastic handles made from cellulose acetate butyrate (CAB) are, in some ways, superior to those made from wood and often provide a firmer and more comfortable grip than do wooden handles. They are also firmly fixed to the steel of the blade and never come off.

Pump and ratchet screwdrivers make the driving of screws easier and quicker. The 'Yankee' type pump screwdriver, made in four sizes – heavy, medium, light and 'Handyman' – each with a number of different screwdriver blades, can save considerable time and effort when a large number of screws have to be driven or removed. The chucks of pump screwdrivers are designed to hold not only screw bits for slotted screws, but also bits for Pozidriv screws, countersunk bits and bits for boring screw holes. These tools are not revolved in the usual clockwise and anti-clockwise directions, but the screws are revolved by pushing the handle up and down in a 'pumping' action. Helical devices within the tool transform the pump action into a revolving one. The pump action can however be locked when it is necessary to use the screwdriver in a normal, non-pump action.

Ratchet screwdrivers are of value when working in awkward places, such as when hanging doors. The ratchet device enables the tool to be used left-handed or right-handed equally well.

Tools for boring holes

Cutting circular holes of various diameters is an important part of working in wood. Holes will need to be bored to receive screws and bolts, to hold fittings, occasionally for nails, to hold dowels, for decorative effects and for many other purposes. Despite the now widespread use of power drills with their accessories designed for boring holes, two hand tools – a hand drill and a carpenter's brace (see Figs 3.43 and 3.44) – can be regarded as essential tools. These two tools are designed for holding 'drills' and 'bits' in their 'chucks'. Some of the more commonly used drills and bits are illustrated in Fig. 3.45. Bradawls of various sizes are also useful tools for boring holes, particularly when screwing and/or nailing.

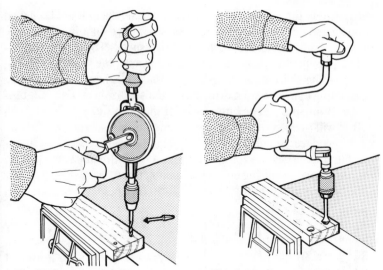

Fig. 3.43   A hand drill   **Fig. 3.44**   A carpenter's brace

Most carpenter's braces are fitted with ratchets which enable the brace to be used in awkward positions where a continuous circle or 'sweep' of the tool's arm is not possible. In such positions the ratchet device will allow the brace to be operated with a backwards and forwards movement of the arm, while the chuck turns clockwise or anti-clockwise only. Most chucks of carpenter's braces are made to hold bits with square taper shanks, but these chucks will also hold cylindrical bits, but not so effectively and firmly.

A double pinion hand drill, with a chuck to receive drill shanks of up to 8 mm (⁵⁄₁₆ in) diameter, is sufficient for most purposes where small holes are to be drilled in wood by hand drill. Morse twist drills are made in a wide range of sizes, the woodworker being mainly interested in those ranging from about 1.5 mm (¹⁄₁₆ in) up to 8 mm (⁵⁄₁₆ in), in 1.5 mm (¹⁄₁₆ in) stages. Larger diameter holes are best bored in wood with bits of various types.

Neither of these tools require a great deal of maintenance other than to ensure they are kept clean and stored in a dry place. An occasional drop of oil on the working parts will be needed from time to time to ensure smooth operation.

Drills and bits will require sharpening from time to time. Great care must be taken when sharpening to ensure not only that the tool will cut well, but that it will continue to cut the diameter of hole it is supposed to cut. Morse drills are best sharpened on a small carborundum grinding wheel revolving at a high speed. The original angle of sharpening must be maintained, as also must the slight clearance angle on the sharpening cone. Some practice is needed before the sharpening of Morse twist drills can be satisfactorily carried out, but drill grinding jigs can be purchased for the purpose.

Bits will need careful filing in order to retain sharpness of their working edges. Small saw files or a set of 'Swiss' needle files (small fine files) are necessary for this purpose. Great care must be taken to maintain correct cutting edges when filing bits.

Some common drills and bits are illustrated in Fig. 3.45.

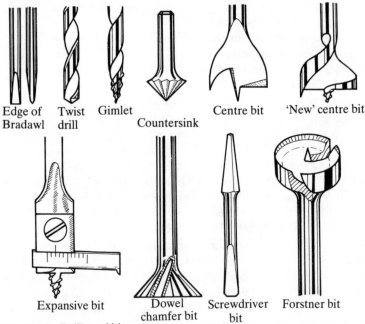

Edge of Bradawl   Twist drill   Gimlet   Countersink   Centre bit   'New' centre bit

Expansive bit   Dowel chamfer bit   Screwdriver bit   Forstner bit

Fig. 3.45 Drills and bits

Bradawl points are similar to the cutting tips of screwdrivers except that the end is sharp, whereas a screwdriver tip must of course be flat.

Twist drills have a cone angle of 120°. High speed steel drills, although more expensive, are tougher and very hardwearing.

Gimlets are not used to any great extent nowadays, but can be useful tools for boring clean holes of diameters from about 3 mm (⅛ in) up to 6 mm (¼ in). Take care to avoid the wood splitting.

Countersink bits are used for shaping the top of a hole ready to receive a countersunk screw.

Centre bits are made in sizes from 10 mm (⅜ in) up to 40 mm (1½ in).

'New' centre bits have a screw which pulls the cutter through the wood as it is bored.

Expansive bits are for cutting large diameter holes. Usually made with two cutters, the smaller for boring holes up to about 30 mm (1¼ in) in diameter, the second for cutting holes up to 75 mm (3 in) in diameter. The position of the cutter can be adjusted in the bit according to the size hole required.

Dowel chamfer bits are for chamfering the ends of dowels to prepare them for jointing purposes.

Forstner bits are for boring holes with a flat bottom. They are available in sizes from 13 mm (½ in) up to 25 mm (1 in).

Twist bits

Twist or auger bits are possibly the most frequently used of the woodworker's range of bits. They are available in a long style, or as shorter dowel bits. Two patterns of twist bits are common. The Jennings pattern is made with two spurs as well as two cutters and also in two types: with a single helical twist or a double helical twist. Jennings pattern twist bits will cut deep holes cleanly and accurately. The Scotch pattern twist bit is for cutting holes quickly and roughly. Scotch pattern twist bits have a coarser thread than Jennings pattern bits. No spurs occur with Scotch twist bits. The cutters of these twist bits are shown in Fig. 3.46.

Fig. 3.46 Jennings and Scotch twist bits

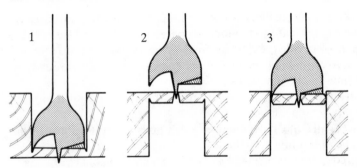

Fig. 3.47 Boring a hole with a centre bit

Spokeshaves

Spokeshaves are tools for smoothing curved edges to their final shape. They are really small planes with a pair of handles. Two types are made. The first has a flat bottom and the second a rounded bottom. The flat sole type is for smoothing convex curves, while those with rounded soles are for smoothing concave ones. Both types work by taking shavings from the wood being shaped. A spokeshave will work more easily if held at a slight angle to the

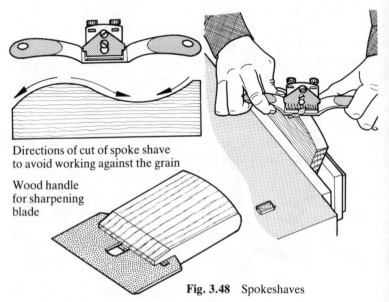

Directions of cut of spoke shave to avoid working against the grain

Wood handle for sharpening blade

Fig. 3.48 Spokeshaves

work, as shown in Fig. 3.48. If held at right angles to the wood, more power is needed by the fingers to push the tool over the work. A smear of candle wax on the sole of the spokeshave will assist in smooth running of the tool. When shaping an edge with this tool, you must make sure you are not working against the grain. Working with the grain avoids bad tearing of the work edges as they are shaped. The blades of spokeshaves are short and hence difficult to hold when being sharpened on an oilstone. A block of wood which can be held firmly in the hands and also hold a spokeshave blade will overcome this problem. Fig. 3.48 shows such a blade sharpening holder.

Rasps and files

Rasps, Surform tools and wood files form a group of hand shaping tools, within which there is a great variety of shapes and sizes. Wood rasps are available with either flat, half round or round sections and are used for rough shaping prior to filing. Surform tools are made in various shapes; some are shown in Fig. 3.50. Surform tools, like rasps, are used for the rough shaping of wood before filing to a finished shape. A group of files such as that illustrated in Fig. 3.50, showing a half round, a flat, a triangular (three square) and a round (rat tail) file, make a useful addition to the woodworker's tool kit. Those shown have plastic handles moulded on to the file tangs. Loose handled files can also be obtained for shaping wood.

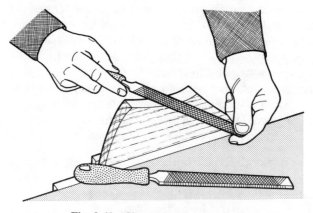

Fig. 3.49 Shaping with a wood file

Rasps and files should be stored in such a manner that the working parts do not rub against each other. They should either be hung or placed in boxes in which partitions prevent contact between the blades. A wire brush – a 'file card' – should be at hand to clean the teeth of files as they become clogged with wood waste. The blades of Surform tools are replaceable when they become worn out with use.

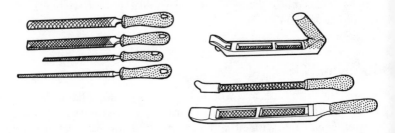

Fig. 3.50 Files and Surform tools

Cabinet scrapers

A cabinet scraper is a thin, flat piece of carbon tool steel, generally about 100 mm long by 75 mm wide (4 in by 3 in). Its two longer edges are burred to provide cutting edges for scraping the surface of wood. Cabinet scrapers are only suitable for the scraping of hardwood. If used on softwoods the surface of the wood will tear. A cabinet scraper can be made from a piece of an old handsaw blade, or can be purchased at a tool shop. The tool is used for scraping out tears and other surface defects left after planing wood and before a final finish is obtained with an abrasive paper. Shaped cabinet scrapers with curved edges are invaluable for cleaning up hollow surfaces in carved work such as a carved dish or a carved bowl. To sharpen a scraper, the procedure is as follows:

1 With a smooth file, file both long edges straight and square.
2 Polish the two filed edges on the edge of an oilstone. Avoid damaging the stone with the thin scraper edges.
3 Polish the scraper sides on the oilstone.

4   Using a scraper burnisher or the rounded back of a gouge, and holding it at a slight angle, rub the two edges of the scraper with firm pressure to form small burrs. This produces four cutting or scraping edges on the two long edges.

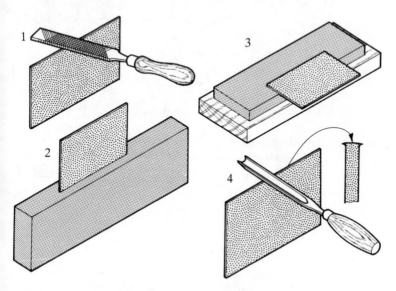

Fig. 3.51   Processes of sharpening a cabinet scraper

Scratch stock

One tool which can prove to be of value when small grooves or mouldings are to be worked on wood, is the home-made scratch stock, illustrated in Fig. 3.52. The stock of the tool is made from any tough hardwood (beech is an excellent choice). Blades are filed, or ground from thin pieces of tool steel. Old machine hacksaw blades are ideal for this purpose. The blades are held firmly within the tool when the wood screws of the stock are tightened. When in use, the tool is worked along the wood so that waste wood is scraped away. The action of the tool is therefore not a true cutting action. Because of the scraping action of the cutter, the sharpening angle should be between about 70° and 80°. Sharpening is carried out by grinding or filing, and then honing with oilslips. Scratch stocks are only suitable

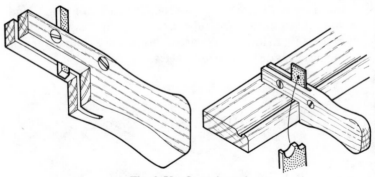

Fig. 3.52 Scratch stock

for working with hardwoods. When used on softwoods, the scraping action of the blade tends to tear out the wood fibres and not produce the exact shape required.

4

Power Tools

Introduction

Hand-held power tools are of increasing interest to woodworkers. These tools are powered by small, but efficient, electric motors which can be connected via cables to a household mains supply. The motors of these tools are designed to function on 50 cycle alternating current (AC), operating at around 240 volts. Their cables are usually connected to a fused plug with rectangular pins, which can be fitted into standard 13 amp mains sockets. If 13 amp sockets are not available as power supply outlets, 15 amp sockets which take round-pinned plugs are quite suitable. The plugs by which hand power tools are connected to the mains electric supply should preferably be fitted with 13 amp fuses. Hand power tools are now available which can be used for drilling, sawing, sanding, grinding, planing and turning.

Hand power tools can have some advantages over hand tools. Much of the hard work involved in operations such as hand sawing, planing, drilling and sanding, can be considerably lessened if power tools are used in the place of hand tools. The power of electricity is used in place of the power of human muscle. Power tools work considerably faster than do hand tools and so a lot of time is saved. Properly used, for suitable operations, some power tools can ensure very accurate work, in producing square edges, straight holes and so on. However, the availability of hand power tools does not lessen the need to acquire skill in using hand tools if you wish to produce good quality craftsmanship.

The most common of modern hand power tools is the power drill. This is a powerful tool to which many attachments can be added to enable operations other than drilling to be carried out. Although modern attachments and accessories designed to increase the range of work which can be carried out by power drills are efficient, woodworkers who intend using power tools to any great extent would be well advised to consider the purchase of separate power tools, each designed for a specific operation.

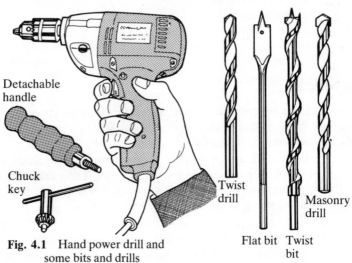

Detachable handle

Chuck key

Twist drill

Masonry drill

Fig. 4.1 Hand power drill and some bits and drills

Flat bit   Twist bit

Power drills

At the present time a wide range of hand power drills are available. Some are designed for do-it-yourself work, some for the home woodworker and some for industrial work. The do-it-yourself and home worker drills are efficient tools, but industrial power drills are designed for continuous, prolonged working under severe conditions. As a result, industrial power drills are more expensive. The woodworker who wishes to put his tools to the maximum use may well consider the extra expense to be fully justified. Power drills of different sizes can be purchased fitted with chucks designed to receive drills either of up to 6 mm (¼ in) shanks, or up to 10 mm (⅜ in) shanks or up to 13 mm (½ in) shanks. The larger types are possibly more versatile, as they will allow heavier work to be carried out.

The majority of power drills are fitted with 'Jacobs' chucks, in which the opening and closing of the three jaws of the chuck is operated with the aid of a toothed key which fits a geared ring on the outside of the chuck. The use of the key allows sufficient pressure to be exerted on the chuck's jaws as they are closed to ensure the jaws hold drills quite securely. Some power drills are supplied with both large and small chucks, which can be unscrewed from the drill spindle. This can be carried out by inserting the chuck key in its hole in the chuck and giving the key shaft a smart blow with a hammer to make the chuck rotate anti-clockwise. Chucks may also have to be removed from the drill spindle in order to allow attachments or accessories to be screwed on the drill spindle.

Power drills can be purchased to operate at a single speed, or with a two, or multiple speed device. If the tool is to be used for such work as drilling in concrete or drilling holes in metal, a two, or multiple speed unit is preferable. Heavy drilling of hard materials requires a slow drill spindle speed, whereas drilling into wood requires a fast spindle speed. Drills can be purchased with a hammer device which when drilling holes into concrete produces hundreds of blows per minute down the spindle on to the drill at the same time as it rotates. Hammer drilling of concrete is far easier than normal drilling. Some hammer drills allow not only the hammer device to be switched in, but can also be run without the hammer action.

Most hand power drills are provided with a detachable side handle which can be screwed into purpose-made screwed holes each side of the power drill casing. As it is advisable to use both hands as often as possible on a power drill when it is being used, the handle should be in frequent use. Not only is it safer to use both hands, because then one of them cannot be damaged by the tool, but then you have more control over its cutting action.

Drills and bits

Of the many different types of drills and bits designed to fit into a power drill chuck for the boring of holes, four of the most commonly used are illustrated in Fig. 4.1.

Twist drills are really designed for boring holes in metal, but are now used extensively for working in wood. They are made in either carbon tool steel or high speed steel. If carbon tool steel heats up, its temper and hardness can be lost and the drill then becomes virtually useless. High speed steel drills will, as their name implies, work at high speeds. If they then become hot, their hardness and temper is unaffected. Thus, although more expensive, high speed steel drills are advisable for use with power drills. A suitable range of twist drills for a woodworker would be: 1.5 mm, 2 mm, 3 mm, 5 mm, 6 mm, 8 mm, 10 mm, 13 mm ($\frac{1}{16}$ in, $\frac{3}{32}$ in, $\frac{1}{8}$ in, $\frac{5}{32}$ in, $\frac{3}{16}$ in, $\frac{7}{32}$ in, $\frac{3}{8}$ in, $\frac{1}{2}$ in).

Flat bits, also referred to as 'slickbits', are excellent for boring larger holes, i.e. up to about 38 mm ($1\frac{1}{2}$ in). These bits will bore holes in wood rapidly, but there will be a tendency for the holes to become out of true when you are cutting deep holes. This can be avoided if the power drill is held in a benchstand, but this is not always possible. Note that power drill bits do not have screwed tips, as the screws could not possibly pull the bits through the wood at the high speeds generated by the power drill. Flat bits vary in size from 10 mm ($\frac{3}{8}$ in) up to 38 mm ($1\frac{1}{2}$ in) in 3 mm ($\frac{1}{8}$ in) stages.

Wood twist bits are used in power drills and are made in sizes from 6 mm ($\frac{1}{4}$ in) up to 13 mm ($\frac{1}{2}$ in) by 1.5 mm ($\frac{1}{16}$ in) stages. They will bore accurate deep straight holes.

Masonry drills are twist bit drills with cutting tips brazed on the end. The tip is made from durium – a hard, very tough, high speed material, hard enough to cut into cement without becoming softened by overheating. They are designed for boring holes in such building materials as brick, wall plasters, cement and so on.

Drill attachments and accessories

Among the many different forms of attachments and accessories available for use with a hand power drill, the following are available:

Drill bench stands hold the power unit in an exactly vertical position so that the drill can be operated downwards under the action of a lever. This ensures not only a powerful leverage pressure on the drill when boring hard materials such as metals, but also ensures accurate vertical drilling.

Orbital sanders are devices to which sandpaper can be fitted and which provide a rotary motion to the sanding in tiny circles of about 3 mm (⅛ in) diameter.

Circular saws are attachments to hold a saw of up to about 125 mm (5 in) diameter.

Jig saw attachments provide vertical reciprocatory up and down movement for jig saws.

Turning devices are made in the form of a light-weight lathe bed into which the power drill can be fitted to provide rotary movement to wood so that it can be turned. Faceplate and dead centre fittings are included with the attachment.

Grinding devices allow a carborundum grinding wheel to be fitted and the power unit held in a form of cradle.

Plastic laminate cutters are heads fitted in the place of the drill chuck, to cut either plastic laminate sheet or thin sheet metal. They cut along curves or straight lines by a 'nibbling' action.

Safety precautions when using power drills

1 Ensure the drill is tightly held in the chuck.
2 If using an attachment, make certain that it is correctly and firmly attached to the power unit.
3 Hold or cramp the work being drilled very firmly.
4 Use waste wood under work being drilled to avoid damage to the workbench top.
5 Use two hands on the power drill if possible, preferably one hand on the main handle and the other on the detachable handle.
6 Keep the cable lead as short as possible.
7 Loop the cable over your shoulder if possible.
8 Apply firm steady pressure, just sufficient for the work being carried out. Do not exert unnecessary force.
9 Drills and cutters must be sharp and clean.
10 When changing bits or attachments, switch off and disconnect the cable plug from the mains socket.

Hand power jig saw

Fig. 4.2 shows a typical self-powered hand jig saw, which is not an attachment for fitting to a power drill, but designed solely for jig sawing. Such a saw will cut curved or straight lines in hardwoods up to 25 mm (1 in) in thickness. A variety of different blades of various tooth shapes and sizes (for cutting wood, metal or plastic) are available. When sawing with this tool, the following rules should be observed:

1 Ensure the work being cut is firmly held, remembering that the saw cuts on its up stroke.

2 When sawing veneered material (plastic laminate or wood veneered sheets) if masking tape or Sellotape is stuck over the lines to be cut, the veneer will not fray or fracture along the saw cut.

3 When sawing an internal shape, begin by boring a hole into which the blade can be fitted to start sawing.

4 When cutting into a corner, saw into it from both sides to obtain a sharp angle (see Fig. 4.8).

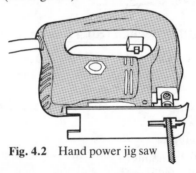

Fig. 4.2   Hand power jig saw

Hand power circular saw

A typical hand power circular saw is shown sawing along a board in Fig. 4.3. Such a saw is fitted with a depth stop device which enables its depth of cut to be adjusted and is also fitted with a fence by which the distance of its cuts from an edge can be set. This type of power tool varies in size, from one which will take a saw of 125 mm (5 in) in diameter up to one with a 200 mm (8 in) diameter saw blade. Larger tools taking blades up to 380 mm (15 in) diameter, are made for industrial use. A rule of thumb by which one can assess the thickness of material which such a saw will cut through, is that the depth of cut is approximately one-third of the saw diameter. Thus a 125 mm (5 in) saw will cut through wood of a thickness of about

40 mm (1⅝ in). However smaller saws, with their inevitably smaller power units, need slow and careful use if maximum sawing thickness is to be achieved.

Fig. 4.3 Hand power circular saw

Saw blades

Of the different types of saw blades on sale, three are shown in Fig. 4.4.

General purpose blades are for cutting down or across the grain. They have four to six points to the inch (4 to 6 mm pitch). The angle between the teeth is 60°, and they are set as for a handsaw.

Rip saws have larger teeth, as shown in Fig. 4.4. The teeth are set as for a handsaw, and are larger – from pitch of 13 mm (½ in) to 30 mm (1¼ in) – on saws designed for hand power tools.

Tungsten carbide tipped saws have each tooth tipped with a tungsten carbide inset, brazed to the saw. The teeth are large, about 30 mm (1¼ in) pitch, and designed for cutting continuously without need to re-sharpen. There is no set and the blades are hard steel. When sawing materials such as chipboard, tungsten carbide tipped saws avoid the need for repeated sharpening.

Other types are gulletted saws for very rapid cutting. 'Planer' saws, of hard steel, with specially shaped teeth and fine toothed saws, for cutting sheet metal such as aluminium.

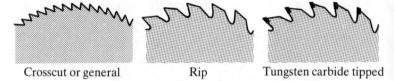

Crosscut or general   Rip   Tungsten carbide tipped

Fig. 4.4   Three different circular saw teeth

Uses for circular saws

The main value of powered circular saws is their ability to saw pieces of wood rapidly to the required width and length. They are designed to cut only along straight lines. With experience, and with the aid of a saw bench into which a portable circular saw can be fitted, a circular saw can be employed for cutting rebates and grooves and also for sawing tenons, bridle joints, halvings and housings. With adequate jigs, there is no need even to fit the saw into a saw bench. If you possess a non-portable circular saw bench, complete with its own fence and saw depth adjusting device, all these forms of sawing – rebating, grooving and some jointing – are possible.

Safety precautions for circular saws

All power driven saws are potentially very dangerous. Severe accidents have resulted from incorrect and improper use. Precautions such as the following must be observed.

1   Saws must be kept sharp and, if necessary, correctly set.
2   Saws must be firmly tightened on to their saw spindles.
3   All guards must be always in position and in correct adjustment.
4   If using a saw bench, its riving knife must be correctly fitted. The purpose of a riving knife is to keep open the saw cut behind the saw blade, to prevent the saw cut binding on the blade if it closes.
5   When using a portable hand circular saw, adjust the depth of cut so that the blade just cuts through its necessary thickness.
6   Ensure that the area underneath the wood being cut is free to allow the saw to poke through without damage to either material or persons.
7   If using a bench saw, a 'push' stick (see Fig. 4.5) will prevent hands being near to the saw as it revolves.

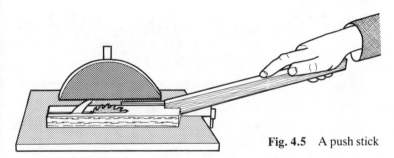

Fig. 4.5 A push stick

Power sanders

Three types of hand power sander are made. These are disc sanders, orbital sanders and belt sanders. In disc sanders, a circular piece of sandpaper is revolved on a flexible backing. In orbital sanders, the sandpaper is made to revolve in tiny circular movements no more than about 5 mm in diameter. In belt sanders, a continuous belt of sanded material (usually on a cloth backing) is revolved over two drums. Although we are concerned here only with orbital sanders, a disc sander as an accessory to a hand power drill may be of value for some work. A quick comparison between the three types of machine might be of value:

Disc sanding is good for rough shaping or for the first stage of smoothing a rough surface. Circular disc sanding marks are difficult to remove from a flat surface. When in use, one must keep working the disc over the whole surface being sanded.

Orbital sanding is excellent general purpose sanding for flat surfaces, by a machine (see Fig. 4.6). Good, clean, smooth and almost mark-free surfaces are produced. Work slowly from place to place over the whole surface being sanded.

Belt sanding is frequently used in industrial practice, but not so common among amateur woodworkers. Excellent smooth surfaces are produced, providing the belt is not allowed to stay in any one position for too long.

The most frequently used sandpaper for machine sanding is that made with aluminium oxide grit. Four grades are common when working on wood. These are:

Coarse	60 grit
Medium	80 grit
Fine	100 or 120 grit
Very fine	150 grit

When working with sanding machines, some general rules should be observed:

1 Great pressure is not needed. Apply only sufficient pressure to allow the grit of the sandpaper to work efficiently.
2 Take care to avoid the rounding of edges and corners.
3 Start with coarse grade papers and progress down to fine grades.
4 Make certain that the sandpaper is firmly held in its machine.
5 Keep a disc sander moving all the time, keep an orbital sander moving slowly and do not allow a belt sander to make bad score marks along the grain by allowing it to stay in one place too long.

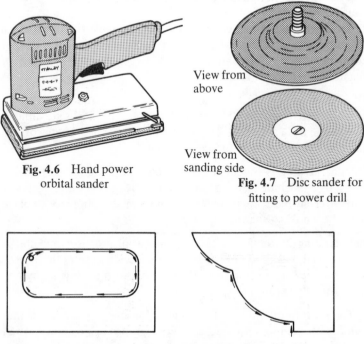

Fig. 4.6 Hand power orbital sander

View from above

View from sanding side

Fig. 4.7 Disc sander for fitting to power drill

Fig. 4.8 Sawing holes and curves by jig saw

Other power tools

Four other power tools will be touched upon briefly here. These four tools are less common than those previously described.

Planers Several firms produce powered hand planers. These are often fitted with 70 mm wide cutters consisting of a rotating cylinder on which two or three cutting blades are fixed. The blades can be removed for sharpening and can be adjusted for depth of cut. The bodies of power planers are fitted with a fixed back sole and a front sole which can be adjusted up and down vertically to produce a heavy or a light cut. Fences and depth stops are also fitted to enable the tool to be used for rebating.

Bandsaw Fig. 4.9 is a diagrammatic illustration showing the operation of a bandsaw. A continuous strip of saw of as little as 6 mm wide (although much wider saws are used on larger machines) runs continuously over two wheels. The saw is held and runs against some form of roller guide and work is pushed against the saw, on a saw table. Bandsaws can be employed for a very wide range of operations and, in skilled hands, are versatile power tools. They can be used for sawing along straight lines and curved lines and various forms of jointing. Perhaps the greatest advantage of bandsaws is that they achieve the maximum depth of cut for a minimum of power. Even with small bandsaw machines, with, say, 300 mm (12 in) diameter pulleys, cuts of up to 75 mm (3 in) can be made. This is because the narrowness of the blade reduces friction to a minimum.

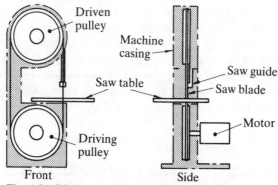

Fig. 4.9 Diagrammatic drawing of a jig saw

Routers contain a vertical spindle which is driven at very high rotational speeds by an electric motor. A number of different cutters can be fitted on the end of the spindle. The cutting ends of the tools protrude below a small table set under the power unit and this table is adjustable for height. Two large handles can be held each side of the machine so that it can be moved over the surface of the wood as it is worked. Grooves, patterns, lettering, backgrounds to relief carvings, are some of the functions which can be performed by routing.

Lathes and turning will be dealt with later (see pages 158–166).

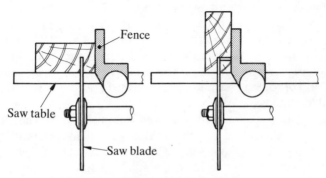

Fig. 4.10   Rebating with a circular saw

Safety

All tools which cut wood are potentially dangerous. Power driven machines are much more dangerous than hand tools because their cutters move at great speed. In particular, all wood cutting power saws should be regarded as dangerous and should be used with an eye to the damage they are capable of causing. Unless due regard is paid to safety precautions, you may well find yourself in a situation where a machine is inflicting damage on a person or on material before you have time to switch it off.

Some general safety rules

1   Ensure plugs are correctly wired (see Fig. 4.11). The international colour coding system for wiring plugs is:

Live (L)   – Brown
Neutral (N)   – Blue
Earth (E)   – Green

L, N and E are usually marked on the plug. If a plug is wrongly wired, it is possible for the operator of a tool connected to the plug to become electrocuted.

2 Solder ends of leads. This produces stronger connections to plugs.

3 Fuses should be at correct rating (usually 13 amps for hand power tools).

4 Understand the tool. Read the instructions. Follow them completely.

5 Loose clothes should not be worn. Loose long hair should be held back in cap or net.

6 Cables should run over shoulders if possible.

7 Wear protective goggles and dust masks if working on some materials for long periods of time.

8 Make sure that lighting is good. You must be able to see the tool and the work clearly.

9 Keep waste cleared away. Some powered machines generate a great deal of waste in the form of sawdust, shavings or chips, very quickly. If not cleared away, such accumulations can be very dangerous.

10 Water or damp must not come into contact with electrical parts.

11 Make sure the work being cut is firmly secured.

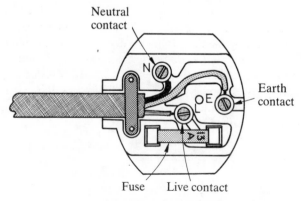

Fig. 4.11 Wiring a 13 amp plug

Multiple power tools

Some mention should be made here of multiple purpose woodworking power tools. Several firms make very successful machines which can be adjusted to saw, plane, sand, mould and perform other machine operations. Some of these multi-purpose machines could be of particular interest to the home woodworker who wishes to indulge in the craft as a hobby. The firms who design and produce such machines are always ready and willing to provide literature or give demonstrations of their machines when approached.

5

Workshop Equipment

Benches and bench equipment

Although a great deal of working in wood is carried out without the aid of benches, sooner or later one will be required and the majority of woodworkers will eventually need to have access to a bench. Many woodworkers in fact do all of their craft work on benches. A bench may be an old table fitted with some form of vice or a thick wide board of wood fixed to a wall at the back and supported by legs at the front. A woodwork vice, in which pieces of wood can be firmly held while they are worked, is almost essential for those who wish to practice the craft seriously. Purpose-made benches can be purchased.

Two benches are illustrated in Fig. 5.1, both of which have been designed and made by the author. The first is a very simple construction, which could be made by a person with minimal skills. The second is a more complex construction, requiring a high degree of skill and was really designed for use by a cabinet maker. The more simple of these two benches consists of four legs to which rails have been glued and screwed. On this framework a bench top has been fixed, with strips of wood screwed inside the frame and to the underside of the top. A hardwood was used throughout, but the legs and framing could have been made from redwood. It is advisable to have a hardwood bench top, in order to withstand the considerable wear to which it will be subjected. Woodwork vices have been fitted to both benches.

When choosing a woodwork bench, check that the height of its top is suited to your own personal height. A tall person of, say,

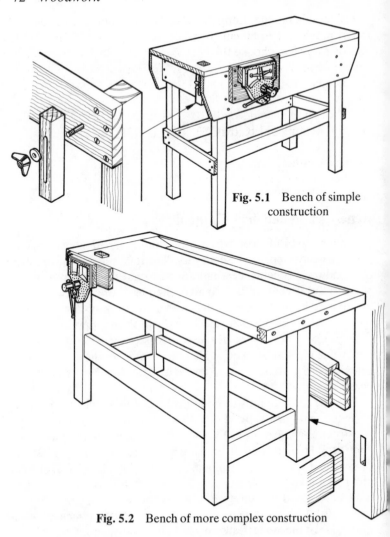

Fig. 5.1 Bench of simple construction

Fig. 5.2 Bench of more complex construction

1 m 80 cm (6 ft), needs a bench about 840 mm (33 in) high, whereas a shorter person of, say, 1 m 70 cm (5 ft 7 in) would need a bench about 760 mm (30 in) high. The discomfort of working at a bench which is too high or too low for long periods of time can cause

considerable fatigue. Lengths can vary from about 1 m 20 cm (4 ft) to as much as 1 m 80 cm (6 ft), or even longer if desired. When choosing a vice, choose the best and largest which you can afford. Some form of quick release device for the vice jaws is an added advantage, as this saves time and avoids frustration. If the vice is made from metal, always fit it with wooden jaws. A planing stop fitted at the left-hand end of the bench, to hold wood against a planing action, is also advisable.

Sawing trestles

Although manufactured trestles such as the 'Workmate' are very versatile, mainly because they convert to a small bench in addition to their value as sawing trestles, a pair of wooden trestles such as shown in Fig. 5.3 are a very useful addition to your equipment. They will prove to be of value when large boards require sawing, particularly material such as sheets of manufactured boards. Sawing trestles are probably best made from a tough hardwood such as beech, but if the legs and rail are made from redwood and the top from hardwood, trestles will last for many years of heavy usage.

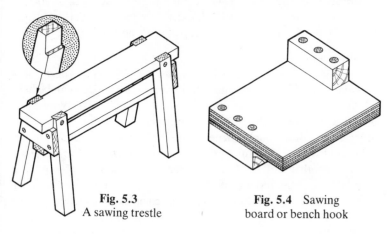

Fig. 5.3
A sawing trestle

Fig. 5.4 Sawing
board or bench hook

Sawing board

One of the commonest and most valuable of items of bench equipment is a bench hook or sawing board. A sawing board like the one shown in Fig. 5.4 does not take long to make. Note that the board itself is made from thick plywood, which will last many more years than the more usual thick 'solid' wood board. Sawing boards should be dowel jointed and glued as shown. If screws hold the parts together there is always the danger that the saw will run through on to a screw, and so blunt the saw teeth.

Mitre box

Another valuable piece of bench equipment is a mitre box for sawing the 45° cuts of mitred frames such as picture frames. It is essential these boxes are made from tough hardwoods and that the 45° sawcuts are accurately cut. If made from softwood, there will be some doubt as to whether the saw kerfs (in which the saw runs when the box is in use) will remain unworn and accurate.

Shooting board

A shooting board, for planing end grain of pieces of wood accurately square, is another useful item of bench equipment. Two types of board are illustrated in Fig. 5.6. In the first, the wood being 'shot' and the shooting board are clamped together in a vice while the plane runs in the rebates cut in the sides of the piece of equipment. In the second, the wood is shot by moving a plane lying on its side along the board with the right hand, while the left hand holds the piece of wood firmly against the stop of the board (see also Fig. 5.9).

Planing trough

A planing trough (see Fig. 5.7) for planing chamfers on the corners of squares of woods is another simple jig, in which wood can be held while corners are planed. Lengths of square wood can be planed to a cylindrical shape with the aid of a planing trough. First, chamfers are planed along each corner, thus reducing the square to an octagonal shape, then further corners are planed making the piece nearly cylindrical. The final cylinder is obtained by planing the wood as it is repeatedly turned in the trough, with a very finely set plane, followed by sanding.

Oilstone box

Although drawings of oilstone boxes have already been shown on page 32, a box fitted on its own platform for holding in a vice, is illustrated in Fig. 5.8. The platform prevents oil from staining the top of the bench. Once oil gets on to a bench top, it quickly stains pieces of wood being worked at the time.

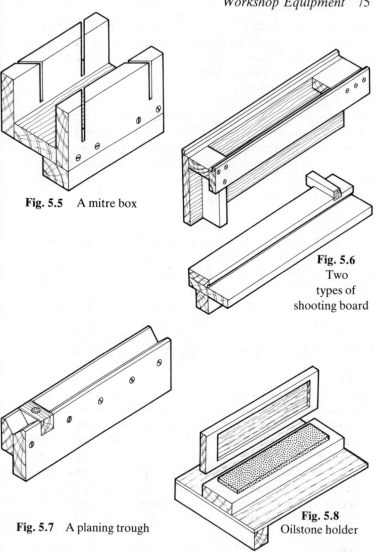

Fig. 5.5   A mitre box

Fig. 5.6
Two
types of
shooting board

Fig. 5.7   A planing trough

Fig. 5.8
Oilstone holder

Note that all the equipment illustrated can be made by the woodworker himself. The best wood for this purpose is beech, but most tough hardwoods will be quite suitable. All parts of the equipment should be jointed with glue and screws or with glue and dowels.

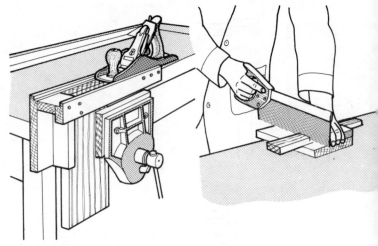

Fig. 5.9 Wood for shooting in a shooting board

Fig. 5.10 Sawing wood with the aid of a sawing board

Cramps

Two major purposes are served by cramping devices. The first is to secure wood being worked so that it does not slip. The second is to hold together wooden parts when they have been glued, to allow the glue to set while the pieces are held firmly together. The most common forms of cramp are woodwork vices, which are attached to the benches at which work is carried on. Other forms of vice of a temporary nature can also be purchased. Such vices are designed to enable wood to be held on, say, a kitchen table, while being worked. All woodwork vices are designed so that wooden jaws can be fitted to their holding faces.

Another common group of cramps are G cramps. These vary in size and can also vary in shape depending on the use for which they have been made. A typical use for a G cramp is shown in Fig. 5.12, where a table leg is shown being held firmly on to a bench top to enable mortises in the leg to be chopped out. Quick-grip cramps are a modified form of G cramp in which the jaw holding the cramping screw can be slid along the cramp bar to allow rapid adjustment of size between jaws. The type shown in Fig. 5.11 is a lightweight quick release G cramp.

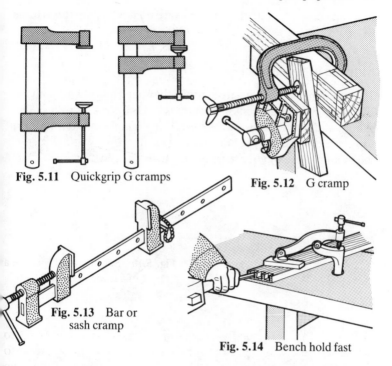

Fig. 5.11 Quickgrip G cramps

Fig. 5.12 G cramp

Fig. 5.13 Bar or sash cramp

Fig. 5.14 Bench hold fast

The bench holdfast, the rod of which is inserted into a hole in a bench top, is designed for holding work firmly and securely on the bench while it is being worked with tools. The leverage of the steel rod against the wooden sides of the hole enables the screw of the holdfast to be adjusted on to the work to hold it very securely in position. A typical example of a holdfast in use is illustrated in Fig. 5.14.

For the gluing and then cramping of frame constructions, bar (or sash) cramps are invaluable. These can be purchased with bars up to 2 m (6 ft 6 in) long and even then extension bars can be obtained to increase that length. A common bar cramp is one with a 1 m (3 ft 3 in) bar.

Note that when using cramps with steel jaws, it is advisable always to place wooden cramping blocks (any piece of waste softwood is suitable) between the wood being cramped and the steel jaws of the cramp itself. This safeguard will prevent the quite severe bruising that can occur when steel cramp jaws are tightened directly on to the wood.

Storage of woodwork tools

To obtain the best service from tools, they need to be kept clean and sharp. Badly maintained or blunt tools do not work as well as they should and can even be dangerous. For example, a blunt tool can slip instead of cutting the line along which it is being worked. Part of the maintenance of your tools is storing them correctly.

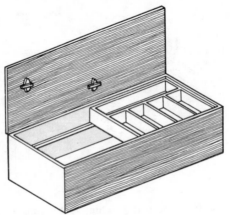

Fig. 5.15   Purpose-made tool box

Where should tools be stored? They can be kept in purpose-made boxes, as illustrated in Fig. 5.15 or in racks, as shown in Fig. 5.16. Wherever they are stored, that place should be set aside for nothing but your tools. Wherever this store is, be it a shed, a room, a special workshop or a cupboard, the best method of storage is to make individual racks for each tool. Such racks can be made from wood, although there are various clips and racks which can be purchased for this purpose. If your woodwork must be carried out in any space available at the time, the best storage method is to make or to purchase a tool box which can be carried from place to place as required. Woodwork tools do not take kindly to metal tool boxes, so wooden boxes are preferable.

Moisture is an enemy to good tool maintenance, as it makes rust

Fig. 5.16 A rack for storing chisels and a rack for saws

form on the surfaces of most steel tools. Rusting can be prevented by placing bags of silica gel crystals or strips of rust-inhibiting paper between tools. No matter how your tools are stored, make it a rule to check that all tools are cleaned and put away in their proper places at the end of each session of woodworking. Many wood-workers also prefer to sharpen tools which have become blunt before placing them back in their racks. This means that the tools are ready for immediate use at all times.

6

Constructions

Despite the increased use of metals, plastics and other materials in the manufacture of many articles which were at one time made from wood, there is more wood used today than at any time in history. Those who have worked in a variety of materials will know why this is so. Wood is the most versatile and easily worked of the constructional materials and, what is more, it can be worked with the minimum of tools and special equipment. (Very large structures can be built from wood without special machinery.) On the other hand wood cannot be easily bent, cast, pressed or moulded, as other solid materials can. It also possesses certain weaknesses such as easy splitting along the grain. Because of these qualities and defects special methods of construction have been developed for the making of wooden articles and structures. Some of these methods have been practised for hundreds of years; others are very recent introductions. Methods of construction suitable for both 'solid' wood and manufactured boards are described in this chapter.

Nailing and nailed constructions

The most common method of construction is nailing. Nails can be purchased by weight, at so much per kilogram, half kilogram (1 lb) or quarter kilogram (½ lb). You will also be able to purchase them in small pre-packed quantities. Purchasing by weight is cheaper than buying packeted nails, but only if you are going to use all the nails you buy. For heavy work such as flooring, roof joists, fencing and making of large boxes, the common wire (French) nail is appropriate (see also page 16). The oval nail (or *brad*) is of more value for lighter woodworking. The small heads and the elliptical section of oval nails minimises splitting as the nails are driven into wood. Always place the oval to lie with the grain. Lost head nails are a more modern nail which can be used instead of wire nails. Panel pins are of particular value as their thin pins and small heads make them suitable for much of the light nailing carried out by the home woodworker. Hardboard pins are hardened nails for pinning hardboard to frames. The tough pin can be hammered through board without the pin buckling.

Rules to observe when nailing

Rust, dirt, grease or glue spots on the face (or *pein*) of a hammer head will cause nails to bend as they are driven home. You should clean the face of the hammer on fine sandpaper. Dovetail nailing (see Fig. 6.1) is considerably stronger than straight nailing and should be practised where possible. Nails should be clinched (as shown in Fig. 6.4) when making nailed frames or when nailing up matchboard to frames. If nails are placed in line along the grain, the wood will split as they are hammered home, so stagger the positions of the nails. Several sizes of nail punch, for 'punching' nail heads below the wood surface, make a useful addition to a tool kit. The punch holes can be filled in with putty, wood filler, wood stopper or Polyfilla if you wish.

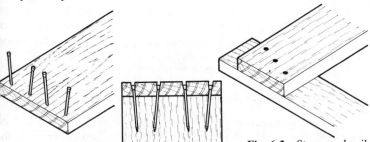

Fig. 6.1 Method of dovetail nailing

Fig. 6.2 Staggered nails in a frame joint

A properly nailed joint is extremely strong and quite satisfactory if used in an appropriate situation. Such joints can be so strong that professional woodworkers often jokingly refer to nails as 'steel dowels'. Badly nailed constructions can be weak and useless particularly when the wood has been split by the nails. This is why the greatest use of nails is in softwoods and they have only limited use in hardwoods.

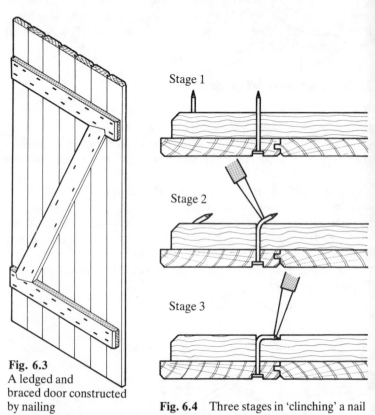

Fig. 6.3
A ledged and braced door constructed by nailing

Fig. 6.4 Three stages in 'clinching' a nail

If a properly made nailed joint is also glued with an appropriate adhesive, then the construction will be very strong and difficult to break. However, not all nailed joints are suitable for gluing.

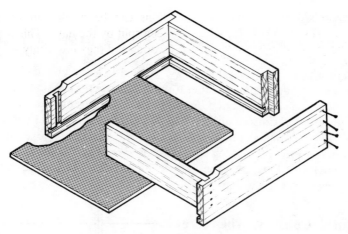

Fig. 6.5   A drawer made by nailing

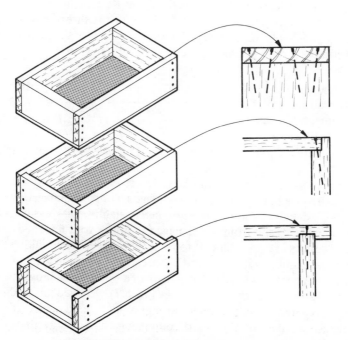

Fig. 6.6   Three methods of making nailed boxes

Screwing

Screwed constructions in wood are very strong and have the advantage that, unless they are also glued, they can be taken to pieces merely by withdrawing the screws. Many articles can be made just by screwing and using no other form of construction. Wood screws are sold in a vast range of different types and different sizes and are made from various materials. The most frequently used sizes are sold in boxes of 200, others in boxes of 100, and some in boxes of 50 screws. More often they are purchased in tens (sometimes in dozens), sold loose over the counter, but then they tend to be more expensive per screw than when they are bought by the box.

Rules to observe when screwing

Always drill holes of the correct size to receive any particular wood screw. If you do not do so, either the wood will split or the screw will fail to hold securely. This normally means three separate drillings. First the shank hole, then the pilot hole for the thread part of the screw and finally, if necessary, the countersinking of the shank hole. Drill sizes for the commonly used gauges of screws are:

Gauge	**4**	**6**	**8**	**10**
Shank drill diameter	3 mm (⅛ in)	4 mm (5/32 in)	5 mm (3/16 in)	6 mm (7/32 in)
Pilot drill diameter	2 mm (1/16 in)	2 mm (3/32 in)	3 mm (⅛ in)	4 mm (5/32 in)

Try to use the correct width of screwdriver blade, as too wide or too narrow a blade will result in damaged wood or damaged screw slots. A damaged screw slot is not only unsightly, but the slivers of metal which result from the damage can injure your fingers. Damaged screws are also difficult to remove. Stagger screws along the grain to minimise splitting and to spread the pressure area of the screws. About two-thirds of the length of a wood screw should be in the lower part of a screwed joint (see Fig. 6.7). Screwed joints which are also glued are probably the strongest of all wood constructions because no part of the wood comprising the joint needs to be removed.

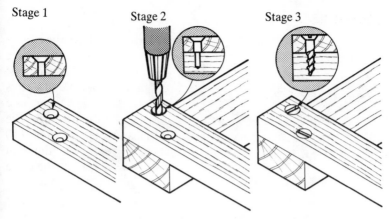

Stage 1 Stage 2 Stage 3

Fig. 6.7 Drill correct size holes when screwing

Fig. 6.8 Use correct width of screwdriver blade

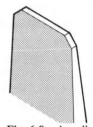

Fig. 6.9 A well sharpened screwdriver tip

Examples of screwed joints

Several methods of using screws in constructional work are illustrated in Fig. 6.10 and Fig. 6.11. Fig. 6.10 shows two methods of jointing box or carcase corners when screws need to be driven into the end grain. Either a dowel fitted across the width of the wood to receive the screws, or fibre plugs set in holes in the end grain, will ensure a good grip for the screws. The fibre plugs should be glued into their holes to increase their capacity to grip. If screws are driven into end grain without such aids, the screw threads rapidly strip the holes and then easily pull out. Fig. 6.11 shows methods of corner

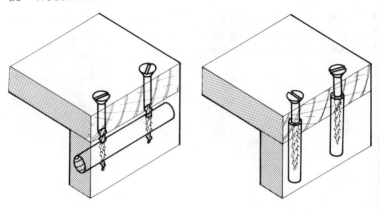

Fig. 6.10 Methods of screwing into end grain

jointing with square strip material screwed to the sides. If the joint is in any form of manufactured board, the strips can be glued and screwed directly in position. If it is in solid wood, only the front end of the strip can be glued and the remainder is screwed through slotted holes. As the solid wood shrinks and expands in relation to atmospheric humidity, so the screws will slide in their slots. The right-hand drawing of Fig. 6.11 shows an added refinement in that the joint is also rebated.

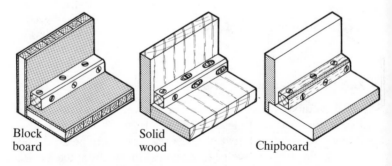

Block
board

Solid
wood

Chipboard

Fig. 6.11 Jointing corners with screwed strips of wood

In Fig. 6.12 a method of edge-jointing boards by screwing is shown. Screw and slot positions are marked as in drawing 1 and then screws are driven in and slots cut, as shown in drawings 2 and 3.

Edges are then glued, screw heads fitted into the 'key-holes' and they are driven home along the slots by hammer blows on the end of the board containing the screws.

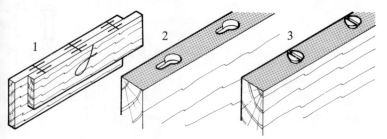

Fig. 6.12 Edge jointing by slot screwing

A blanket chest

To illustrate how a simple item of furniture can be made with an all-screwed construction, Fig. 6.13 shows a simple blanket chest made from chipboard veneered on both sides with a choice hardwood, for example, mahogany. The construction is based on joining all the adjacent edges with 15 mm (⅝ in) square hardwood strips, then gluing and screwing them with chipboard screws at all the corners. The work can proceed in three stages, after preparing all the parts to their correct finished sizes.

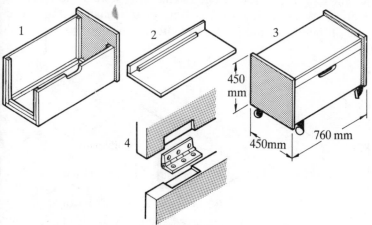

Fig. 6.13 A blanket chest made from veneered chipboard

Stage 1   Glue and screw wood strips to the bottom and to the ends. Then glue and screw through these strips into the back and front. Remember to saw out a handle grip hole in the front with a coping saw and file.

Stage 2   Construct the lid in a similar manner.

Stage 3   Fit and screw at least three 75 mm (3 in) brass butt hinges into slots chiselled into the underside of the lid and the top edge of the back.

Iron matching edging strip in position where necessary. Castors should then be screwed under each bottom corner to allow the blanket chest to be moved easily from place to place.

Halving joints

Many strong framed constructions can be made with halving joints, so named because half of the wood from each of the two parts of the joint is removed by sawing or chiselling. There are three common types: corner halving, Tee halving and cross halving. A fourth type – dovetail halving – will be dealt with later in the section on dovetails (see page 114). Corner halvings often need to be screwed or nailed in addition to being glued. Tee and cross halvings normally only need to be glued. The processes involved in making these joints are shown in Figs 6.15 and 6.16. All three halvings are made either by sawing half of the wood from an end or by sawing and chiselling grooves. When sawing, the saw 'kerf' must be made to the 'waste' side of the line of the joint, as failure to 'saw into the waste' will

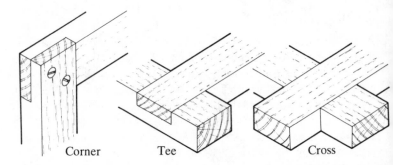

Fig. 6.14   Three types of halving joints

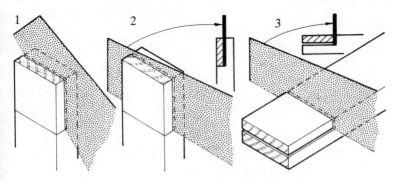

Fig. 6.15 Sawing of part of a halving joint

result in loose joints. When chiselling a halving groove, chisel from both sides of the wood in turn to prevent splitting the back of the groove as the chisel passes across for its final cut.

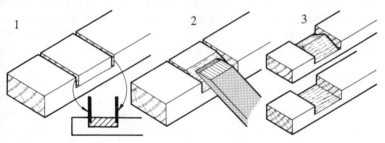

Fig. 6.16 Sawing and chiselling halving grooves

A child's blackboard

A typical framed construction involving halving joints is shown in Fig. 6.17 – a child's blackboard on its own easel. The easel consists of two identical frames joined at the upper corners with corner halvings and centrally with Tee halvings. Both frames are clad with 4 mm thick plywood and the frames then hinged together with a pair of 75 mm (3 in) steel back flap hinges. On top of one of the plywood claddings, 6 mm thick soft pin board could be glued to allow one side of the framework to be used as a pin-up board for the child's art work. Pin board is a soft board into which drawing pins can be easily inserted. Chalk, pencil or brush troughs are glued and pinned both

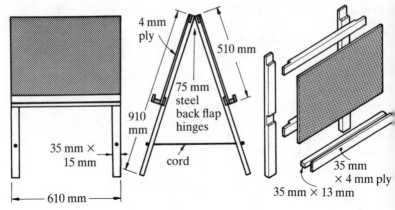

Fig. 6.17 A child's blackboard and easel

sides of the frame. These troughs simply consist of two pieces of wood glued and pinned to each other. The blackboard can be painted black with a matt blackboard paint. A piece of cord fitted through holes between both frames prevents the hinged framework from collapsing when opened out for use.

Housing joints

If you wish to join a shelf to an upright or to a partition, for example in bookracks and bookcases, or if you wish to join partitions to box sides, one of the strongest jointing methods for the purpose is to house one part within the other. Two types of housing joints are shown in Fig. 6.18. These are known as 'through' housings, so called because the groove is cut from one edge of the wood through to the other, and 'stopped' housings, in which the grooves stop short of one of the edges. The processes involved in making both these joints are shown in Figs 6.19 and 6.20. If you wish to make strong, successful housing joints, the grooves must be exactly as wide as the thickness of the wood which is to fit into the groove. To make sure of this, the groove width should be marked directly from the shelf or partition it is being made to hold. You must also 'saw into the waste' when sawing the groove sides. Provided that housing joints are a good, tight fit, needing firm hand pressure to force the shelf into its groove, no nailing should be necessary. It is only necessary to glue the pieces to hold them together strongly and permanently. Stopped housings are more difficult to make than through housings. This is because they require the chopping of a recess into which the saw can be worked when sawing the groove sides. Stopped housings have, however, the advantage that the jointing method cannot be seen from one edge. Dovetail housing joints will be described later in the section on dovetail constructions (see page 114).

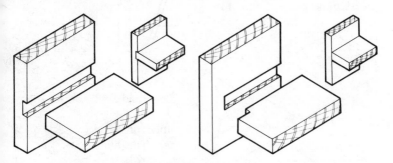

Fig. 6.18   Through housing and stopped housing

Cutting housing grooves

The procedure for cutting grooves for through housings is shown in Fig. 6.19. Groove sides are cut with the saw held vertically on the inside (waste side) of accurately marked groove lines. Some of the waste is removed from between the two saw cuts with a chisel, working from one edge. The wood is then turned round and the groove completed by chiselling out waste from the other edge. At this stage, a router plane, if available, can be used for planing the groove bottom flat and parallel with the surface of the wood.

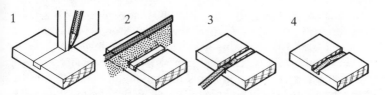

Fig. 6.19   Marking, sawing and chiselling through housing groove

Fig. 6.20 illustrates a method of cutting the groove for a stopped housing. First, a portion of the groove is chopped out with chisel and mallet. This is followed by sawing the groove sides with the front end of a saw, working as far as the chopped-out recess allows. Waste wood is then chiselled to leave the groove bottom flat. Again, a router plane may be used at this stage. It is often necessary to saw away a small portion of the corners of a shelf or a partition to overlap the stopped end of the groove.

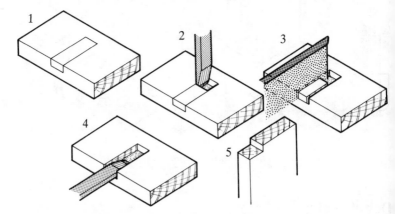

Fig. 6.20 Marking, sawing and chiselling stopped housing groove

A radiator shelf

A shelf above a radiator will give a better distribution of heat flow, as it throws the heat away from the wall. It also prevents the discolouration which occurs above radiators attached to walls (caused by dust carried upwards by convection and settling on the wall). A radiator shelf is an example where stopped housings could be used.

Because of the heat, the shelf must be made from well seasoned hardwood of, say, 22 mm (⅞ in) thickness. Stopped housings are cut at each end on the underside of the shelf to accommodate shaped wood brackets. The shelf can be fixed to the wall by screws into wall plugs set through strips of aluminium, each 30 mm by 19 mm by 4 mm (1¼ in by ¾ in by ³⁄₁₆ in), with holes to take screws into the back of the shelf. Brass mirror plates could equally well be used for this purpose. A good heat-resistant finish could be obtained by applying three brush coats of clear polyurethane varnish. Fig. 6.21 gives sizes suitable for such a shelf; the length depends upon the radiator size. The illustration also shows details of the jointing and the suggested wall fitting strips.

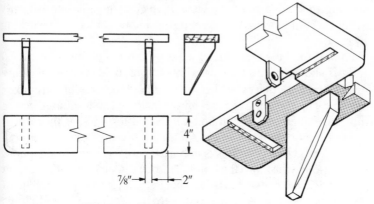

Fig. 6.21 Details of radiator shelf

Dowels and dowelled joints

Dowels are cylindrical lengths of wood which are used either as an integral part of a joint or as constructional members, as in the sides of a cot. They may also be used to provide locating pins to fix the positions of loose or movable parts in items made from wood. Dowels of various diameters from 3 mm (⅛ in) upwards can be readily purchased. These are made from various woods, for example beech, birch or ramin, but any robust hardwood can be used. Woods from which dowels are made should be tough, hard and straight-grained, as well as relatively cheap.

Dowelled joints are easy to make and produce accurate and reasonably strong constructions. The ends of the rails must be square, and flat (preferably planed). Marking out dowel hole positions must be carried out accurately if the joints are to be successful. Proprietory types of dowelling jigs may be used for guiding drills for boring dowel holes. Such jigs ensure that holes line up accurately with their mates and are bored straight and square.

When working with such jigs, a hand power drill fitted with Morse drills can be used, but when working by hand, the best tool for boring dowel holes is the carpenter's brace fitted with dowel bits. If a dowel bit is not available, the next best tool is a twist bit. Drills in a power drill may be used when working without a jig, but there will be a marked tendency for the tips of such drills to wander when starting to bore a hole. However, accurate positioning is easily achieved with the screw point of dowel and twist bits when working by hand.

One of the best methods of marking dowel hole positions for a joint is shown in the four drawings of Fig. 6.22. Gauge lines are marked on both pieces, which are then held together in a cramp or in a vice with the jointing faces upwards. Pencil lines squared across the gauge lines ensure that hole centres correspond, as they are at the intersections of the lines. Another good method for marking joints in awkward positions is to bore the holes in one of the parts, put a little sawdust into the holes, dampen the surface of the second part, and place the two parts together in their jointing position, with the first part on top. A gentle, but sharp, tap with a hammer loosens the sawdust. When the first part is removed, tiny mounds of sawdust

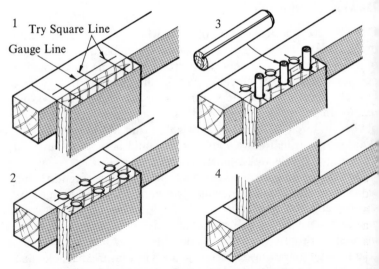

Fig. 6.22 Marking and making a dowelled joint

will indicate the hole positions on the second part. The point of a marking awl or a sharpened nail is then used to stab the centre of each circular mound.

Another useful method, particularly when a large number of identical joints are to be made, is to cut a piece of tinplate to size and pierce holes in it. This is positioned on one part, then inverted on to the second part, and the hole positions are marked through the holes with a pencil or with a steel point. Thick paper or hardboard would also make suitable templates.

After boring the holes for dowels in a dowelled joint, always countersink the hole slightly to allow a small space for glue escaping from the dowel hole. The ends of dowels for jointing should be slightly chamfered at their ends. A saw kerf along the length of joint dowels allows surplus glue to escape when the dowels are glued and driven into their holes.

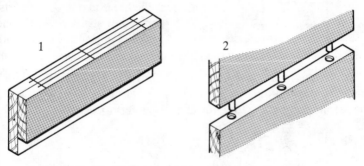

Fig. 6.23 Marking and making a dowelled edge joint

Types of dowelled joints

A variety of different forms of dowelled joints are shown in the illustrations. Fig. 6.22 illustrates the marking out, boring and assembly of a wide rail jointed to a leg. After marking out (1), the dowel holes are bored and slightly countersunk (2). Next, dowels are glued into the holes in the rail end (3), and then the joint can be assembled, glued and cramped. Fig. 6.23 shows the marking out and assembly of an edge joint between two boards. Simple dowelled joints for frameworks are given in Fig. 6.24. This illustration includes a suitable method of jointing rails in a stool, chair or table frame. Note the staggering of dowels and also note that the dowels should be cut to lengths slightly shorter than the depth of the holes into which they are fitted.

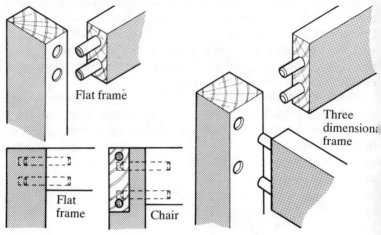

Fig. 6.24 Frame corner joints

Two home-made dowelling jigs are shown in Fig. 6.25. Both are made from wood, the first for making dowels for a framework and the second for making four dowel holes along an edge.

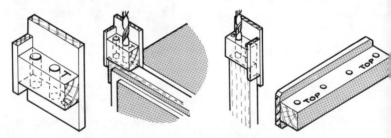

Fig. 6.25 Two home-made dowelling jigs

Jointing manufactured board

Laminated boards – plywoods, batten boards, blockboards and lamin boards – are made on the principle that the grain direction of each layer is at right angles to the grain direction of its neighbour.

Thus as the laminates shrink or expand across their grain, the action is checked by the lack of sympathetic movement in adjacent laminates. Because of this, laminated boards do not change in size as the atmospheric conditions alter, and so they will remain flat unless badly stored. Their composition, with grain alternating in adjacent layers, permits wide boards to be manufactured. Thus panels as wide as 1200 mm (4 ft) and more are readily available and the need to join solid boards along their edges to obtain wide surfaces is eliminated.

These two factors – lack of distortion and availability in wide sheets – are the major reasons for the popularity of laminated boards in woodworking. One big disadvantage, however, is that their edges can be unsightly and may need concealing. There are a variety of methods of 'lipping' edges of manufactured boards, some of which are shown in Fig. 6.26. The method of fixing lippings with loose tongues is very suitable for the home woodworker. So also is the method of using a pre-glued edging strip, which is a narrow length of wood or plastic veneer, treated on one side with a thermoplastic adhesive. The adhesive melts on application with a hot iron and sets hard on cooling.

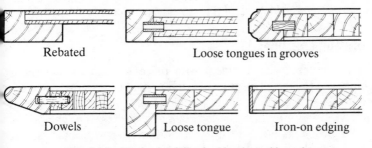

Rebated   Loose tongues in grooves

Dowels   Loose tongue   Iron-on edging

Fig. 6.26 Methods of 'lipping' laminated boards

Four examples of corner joints for manufactured boards are shown in Fig. 6.27. Again the inclusion of loose tongues is possibly the easiest method, as it requires the use of only one special tool, a plough plane. Three of the examples show the use of such loose tongues. The fourth shows a strong corner joint for a three-plywood construction.

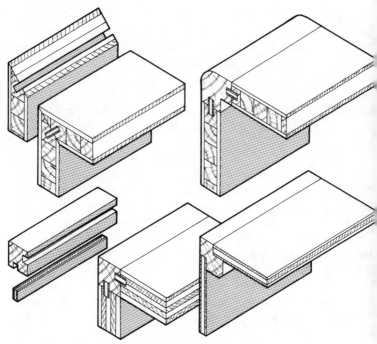

Fig. 6.27   Methods of corner jointing manufactured boards

Jointing chipboards

Because there is no problem with the end grain when jointing chipboard (as the chips are laid at random in the boards), glue can be used along edges cut at any angle. Thus some of the problems involved in jointing 'solid' wood do not arise when using chipboard. Other problems however do occur. First, you will obtain strong joints only if you use adhesives such as the urea-formaldehyde types, the pva types or, when gluing veneers to the surfaces of chipboard, adhesives of the rubber-based impact type. Second, because most chipboards are layered, they are prone to splitting open when you are working into ends or edges. Thus nailing is particularly unsuitable and screwing also must be carried out with care. Some corner jointing methods for chipboard constructions are shown in Fig. 6.28. Other constructions are shown later when 'knock-down' jointing methods are described (see page 100).

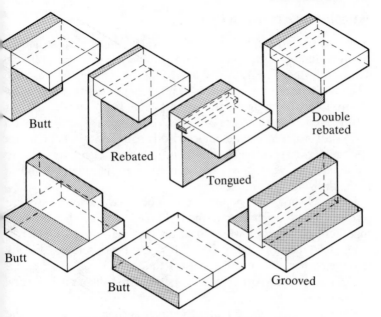

Fig. 6.28   Methods of jointing chipboard

The drawings in Fig. 6.28 show the following constructions which are suitable for chipboard: a butt corner joint, (glued); a rebated, corner joint, (glued); a tongued corner joint (glued); a double rebated corner joint, (glued); a butt partition joint, (glued); a butt edge joint, (glued) and a grooved partition joint, (glued).

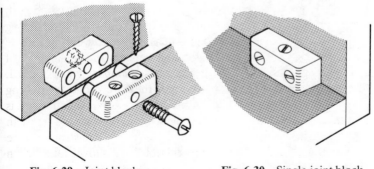

Fig. 6.29   Joint blocks

Fig. 6.30   Single joint block

Knock-down constructions

You may wish to use 'knock-down' or KD methods of construction. Many different types of KD jointing fittings are manufactured and some of the more easily available are illustrated in Figs 6.29 to 6.35. The main value of these modern jointing methods is that they allow strong joints to be made quickly, easily and accurately. Another advantage is that the parts can be speedily taken apart, so that a whole construction can be 'knocked-down' to a flat packet for easy storage or transport. KD jointing methods are particularly suited to chipboard, for which most have been designed. The methods shown in the drawings are as follows.

Fig. 6.29 shows the popular joint block. Two nylon blocks are screwed, one to each face, to the inside of a corner. They are held together by a steel bolt which locks the two boards to each other.

Fig. 6.30 shows a single piece joint block. This is screwed directly into the corners of a box-like construction.

Fig. 6.31 shows a corner joint formed with the aid of a nylon screw plug and a polythene screw cap.

For jointing large KD constructions such as wardrobes, the 'Hafele Rondofix' corner joints might be considered (as in Fig. 6.32).

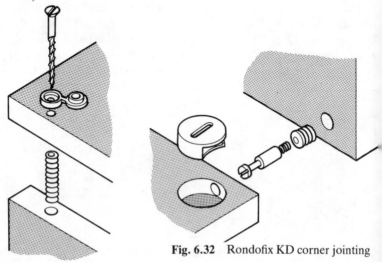

Fig. 6.32   Rondofix KD corner jointing

Fig. 6.31   Nylon screw plug

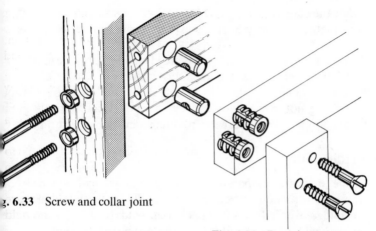

Fig. 6.33 Screw and collar joint

Fig. 6.34 Brass inserts

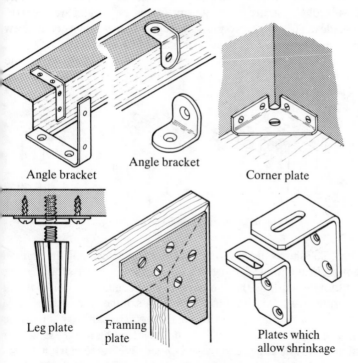

Angle bracket

Angle bracket

Corner plate

Leg plate

Framing plate

Plates which allow shrinkage

Fig. 6.35 Plates and brackets for KD constructions

For the construction of KD frames, steel screw and collar fittings are suitable (see Fig. 6.33) or steel bolts through brass nut inserts, as in Fig. 6.34.

A variety of plates and brackets are also suitable for the making of KD frames or carcases. Fig. 6.35 shows a variety of such plates and brackets. Some of these are designed for use with 'solid' wood containing slots which allow movement of the wood across its grain to take up changes in width due to changes in atmospheric humidity.

Bridle joints

Bridle joints are comparatively easy to work and make good strong frame constructions when well fitted. They have the practical advantage over halvings that each joint holds together without the need for nails or screws. One disadvantage is that the joint is always visible. There are two basic types; the corner and the Tee bridle. Most bridle joints are made at right angles, but not all are necessarily made at 90°, as the two parts of the joint can be at any convenient angle. Corner and Tee bridle joints are illustrated in Fig. 6.36.

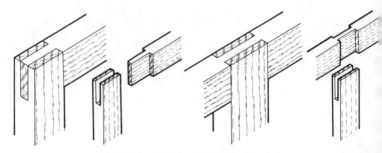

Fig. 6.36 Corner and Tee bridle joints

Fig. 6.37 shows the marking out and the sawing along the grain of a corner bridle joint. A mortise gauge, although not essential, is the best tool for marking the two parallel lines common to both parts of any bridle joint. It is usual to set the points of the mortise gauge to a distance apart equal to one-third of the wood thickness, but this rule is not invariable and may be amended according to the design for which the bridle construction is intended. When the marking out is complete, all sawing must be carried out to the waste side of the

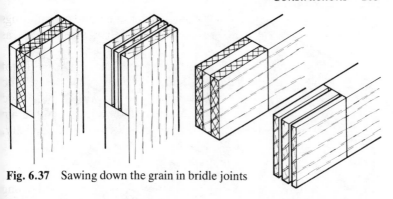

Fig. 6.37 Sawing down the grain in bridle joints

gauge lines, then the waste from the 'open mortises' can be removed with a mortise chisel and mallet, working from either edge of the part carrying the open mortise.

This procedure is illustrated in Fig. 6.38. The waste parts from each side of the tenons of a corner bridle, or from the grooves of a Tee bridle, are removed in a similar way to that used when working halving joints (as shown on page 89).

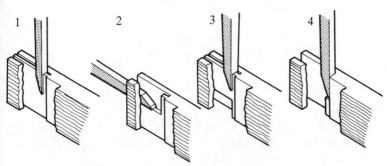

Fig. 6.38 Chopping waste from the open mortise of a bridle joint

The drawings of Fig. 6.39 show two examples of products which could be constructed using bridle jointing. A flush panelled door can be made by constructing a frame with bridle joints and then cladding each face of the frame with plywood or hardboard, glued to the frame. Such doors would normally have the edges 'lipped', but the lippings are not shown so you can see the bridle construction

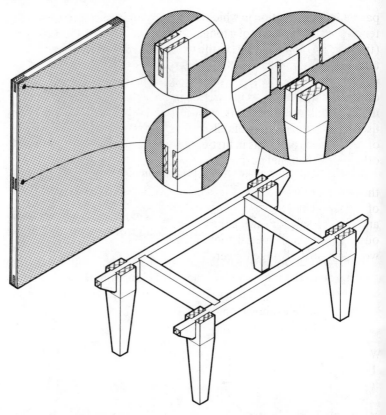

Fig. 6.39   Examples of constructions involving bridle joints

more clearly. The stool frame is another example of bridle joint construction in which the long rails of the stool are fitted into the tops of the legs with Tee bridle joints.

Mortise and tenon jointing

One of the most common of all woodworking joints is the mortise and tenon. If you look around you will find many examples of this constructional method, in furniture and in the construction of buildings. It is a form of jointing capable of a wide number of variations, in fact it is a method which can be adapted to suit the particular construction in which it is being employed. A mortise and tenon consists basically of a tongue (the tenon) which fits into a hole (the mortise). The two parts – the tenon and mortise – must be made to fit each other snugly. It is the accuracy of making these two parts which determines the strength of the resulting joint. The chief uses of mortise and tenon joints are for joining frame members such as the rails and 'stiles' of doors, windows and other flat frames. Other uses include the jointing of rails in chests and wardrobes, the joining of ceiling and roof joists in first-class building practice and countless other constructional purposes.

To make successful mortise and tenon joints, it is advisable to use the correct tools, i.e. a mortise gauge for marking the parallel lines of the tenon and mortise, mortise chisels for 'chopping' the mortise and a tenon saw for sawing the tenon. Good jointing can be carried out without these special tools, but extra skill is needed and the work will possibly take longer.

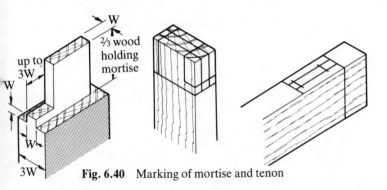

Fig. 6.40 Marking of mortise and tenon

The width (W) of a mortise is usually dependent on the width of the mortise chisel selected for the work (see Fig. 6.40), as the tenon to fit into the mortise must have a similar thickness. Fig. 6.40 showing typical dimensions of a haunched tenon shows that the relationships of the dimensions are based on the width of the mortise chisel employed for cutting the mortise into which the tenon is to fit. The chisel selected for chopping the mortise should normally have a width of about one-third of the thickness of the wood in which the mortise will be cut. Where an exact dimension is not possible, it is best to err on the high side. For example, an 8 mm

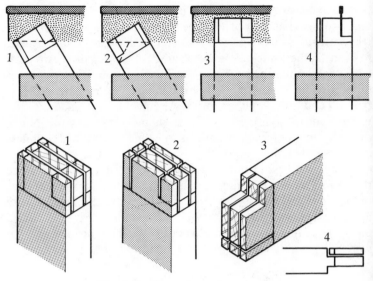

Fig. 6.41   Stages in sawing a tenon

(5⁄16 in) chisel should be used to joint 22 mm (⅞ in) thick wood, and a 13 mm (½ in) chisel to joint 35 mm (1⅜ in) thick wood.

If a mortise is wider than about six times the thickness of the chisel, problems may occur with splitting. When making a stopped tenon, i.e. one which does not go right through the mortised part, its length should be about two-thirds of the width of the mortised member. A longer tenon could result in the mortise being accidentally cut right through and a shorter tenon could produce a weak joint.

Fig. 6.40 also shows how to set out a tenon and a mortise. The haunched mortise and tenon joint illustrated is one which might be employed when making a door, or when jointing a rail into a leg when making a table.

Fig. 6.41 illustrates the stages of sawing a tenon and Fig. 6.42 illustrates the stages in chopping a mortise to take the tenon. Note the 'horn' shown in these drawings. Where a mortise is to be cut at the end of a piece of wood, it is advisable to leave about 25 mm (1 in) of waste beyond the mortise to prevent the wood splitting under the pressure of the mortise chisel, as it is chopped out. Horns

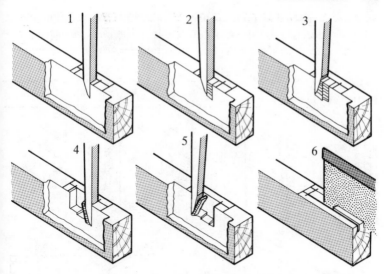

Fig. 6.42   Stages in chopping a mortise

also provide useful extension pieces to take hammer blows when a tightly fitted joint is opened up. These 'horns' are not sawn off until the construction has been glued together.

Six different mortises and tenons are shown in Fig. 6.43. These are only a selection of the large number of different types of this joint which can be made. Those shown are:

1   **A through mortise and tenon** is a joint where the tenon goes right through the upright piece, from edge to edge.
2   **A haunched mortise and tenon**, which here is a 'through' joint, can also be stopped. This is a frame construction joint used for a door frame, for example. The upright piece of a door is known as a *stile* and the horizontal piece as a *rail*.
3   **A double mortise and tenon** is for joining rails sideways to each other.
4   **A barefaced mortise and tenon** is a joint where one side of the piece in which the tenon is cut is not sawn away to form the tenon. An example of the use of this joint is given in the construction of the table on page 109.
5   **A square mortise and tenon** is sometimes referred to as a *stub tenon*.

6 **Jointing a stool or table corner** is done with a haunched mortise and tenon to joint the rails into the leg. The ends of the tenons are 'mitred' at 45°, to ensure a maximum length for the tenon.

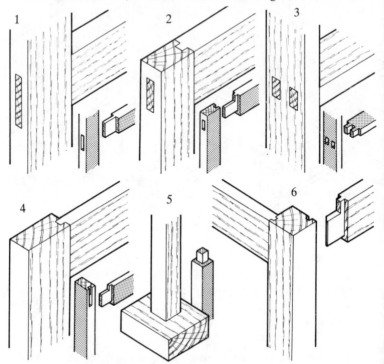

Fig. 6.43 Six mortise and tenon joints

A kitchen table

The construction of a kitchen table is shown in Fig. 6.44. The legs and rails are made from straight-grained, knot-free redwood. The rails are jointed into the legs by means of double haunched mortise and tenon joints. Note the 'staggering' of the tenons into the legs at each corner. The top, of thick, good quality blockboard, is fixed to the frame of the table by means of strips of 22 mm (⅞ in) square wood, glued and screwed into the corners between the rails and the top. The top is veneered with a laminated plastic veneer (such as 'Formica') and its edges are veneered with a white vinyl edging strip, glued in place with a rubber-based impact glue. Dimensions

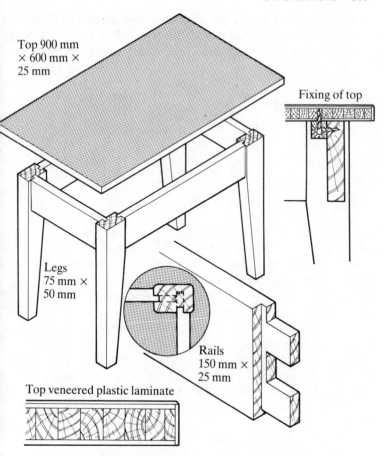

Fig. 6.44 Details of a kitchen table

for the table are: overall height 760 mm (30 in), frame 800 mm by 500 mm (32 in by 20 in) and top 900 mm by 600 mm (36 in by 24 in). The wooden parts of the table frame could be finished by being painted to match the colour scheme of the kitchen.

Dovetails and dovetailing

Of all the joints used by woodworkers, the dovetail is possibly the most effective ever devised. It has been used in a variety of forms by

woodworkers for thousands of years. When accurately made and
bonded with a good adhesive, the dovetail is as strong, if not
stronger, than the uncut wood from which it has been made.

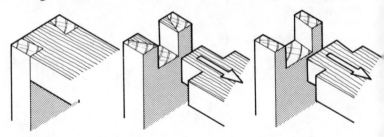

Fig. 6.45   The strength of a dovetail depends on the slope of its 'tail'

Dovetails can be varied in proportion and dimensions to suit the
article for which they are being made, but all are constructed on the
same principle. The strength of a well made dovetail lies in the
shape of the 'tail'. Fig. 6.45 illustrates how a correctly designed
dovetail joint resists pull in the direction of the arrow. The drawings
also illustrate that the angle at which the tail is cut is important, as
too great an angle may cause the tail to split and too small an angle
may allow the tail to pull through. Fig. 6.46 shows effective angles of
slope for general dovetailing. To transfer these slopes to the marking out of a joint, a sliding bevel can be used. Start by squaring a line
across a piece of wood, measure and mark the dovetail slope
required, then set a sliding bevel to the angle. Dovetail templates
(or templets) can be made for the purpose of marking dovetails.
Such a template is shown in Fig. 6.46. Dovetail templates may be
made of wood or metal.

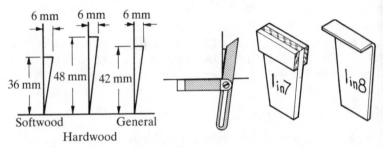

Fig. 6.46   Dovetail slopes. A sliding bevel. Dovetail templates

Two tools which are suitable for dovetailing are the dovetail saw, with its fine teeth and short (200 mm or 8 in) blade, and a set of bevel-edged chisels. The fine teeth of the thin blade of the dovetail saw and the bevels of the chisels are designed for working dovetail joints. The slopes of the bevels will fit neatly into the corners of the parts cut to form the tails.

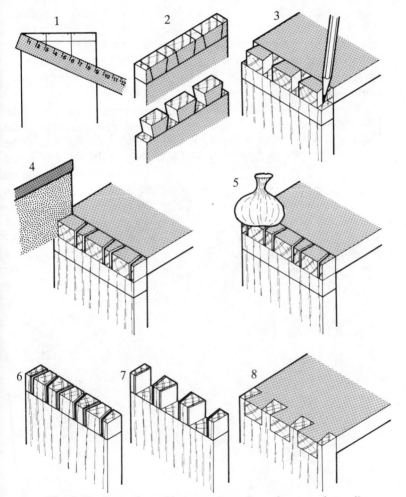

Fig. 6.47 Stages in making a common through corner dovetail

The common corner dovetail

Fig. 6.47 shows a sequence for the cutting of a common through corner dovetail, which would be suitable for the making of boxes of various kinds. The sequence includes three different methods of marking out the 'pins' on the end of the piece into which the tails will be fitted (see drawings 3, 4 and 5). Either a saw can be used, or a pencil, or a pounce bag (a cotton bag filled with chalk). You must decide which method is most suitable. Some woodworkers prefer cutting the pins first, then marking the tails from the pins. In this case, the tails can only be marked from the pins with the aid of a pencil or a scriber point. Whichever method is adopted, well fitted, tight dovetails can only be obtained by 'sawing into the waste' of the marked pins (or tails if the alternative method is used).

Lap dovetail

Fig. 6.48 shows a sequence for the making of a lap dovetail. This form of dovetail is employed in situations where the jointing

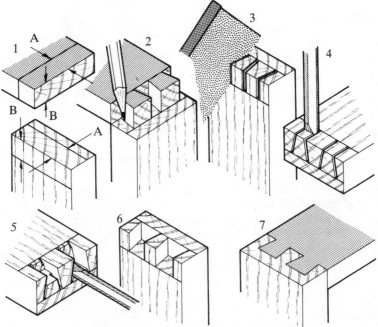

Fig. 6.48   Stages in making a lap dovetail

method should not be visible from one side, as in the case of a drawer front, where traditional drawer sides are joined by a lap dovetail to drawer fronts. Compare the following method of constructing a lap dovetail with that of making a through dovetail. First, the ends of both pieces to be joined should be planed accurately square. A shooting board can be used for this. Shoulder lines are best marked with a cutting gauge. The tails are marked out as for a common dovetail, and then marked on to the part carrying the pins by saw, pencil or pounce bag. It is the cutting of the waste from between the pins which makes this different from the cutting of the common dovetail. After sawing into the waste side of the marked lines at an angle, the waste must be chopped out with chisel and mallet.

Other forms of dovetail joint
Three other forms of dovetail joint are shown in Figs 6.49, 6.50 and 6.51, illustrating sequences of marking out and cutting. These are:

A dovetail housing The drawings in Fig. 6.49 show one type. Other forms include a stopped dovetail housing.

A dovetail halving is shown in Fig. 6.50. Compare with the Tee halving shown on page 88.

A dovetail bridle is shown in Fig. 6.51. Compare with the corner bridle shown on page 102.

Examples of dovetailing
To illustrate a design for which dovetail jointing is eminently suitable, a car tool box is shown in Fig. 6.52. This box, with its tray, will contain most of the tools required by the driver who likes to carry out his own car maintenance and servicing. The box sides should be made from a tough hardwood of 13 mm ($\frac{1}{2}$ in) thickness, the bottom from a hardwood plywood 4 mm ($\frac{3}{16}$ in) thick, and the lid from plywood 6 mm ($\frac{1}{4}$ in) thick.

Another example of typical work for which dovetailing is suitable is illustrated in Fig. 6.53. This shows a traditional construction for making a drawer for a cabinet. Thousands of examples of this form of jointing will be seen in the many drawers found in most homes.

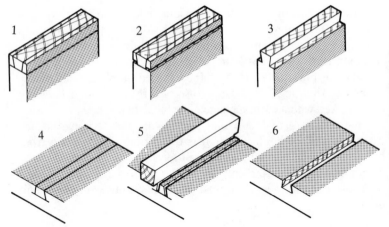

Fig. 6.49 Marking and cutting a dovetail housing

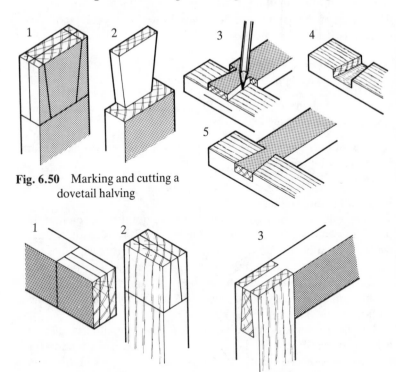

Fig. 6.50 Marking and cutting a dovetail halving

Fig. 6.51 Marking and cutting a dovetail bridle

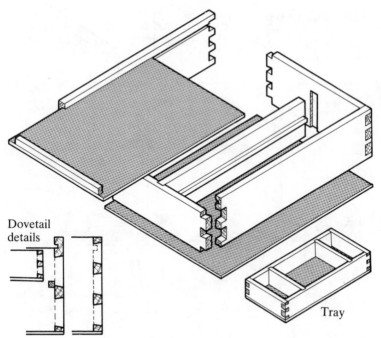

Dovetail details

Fig. 6.52 A car tool box

Tray

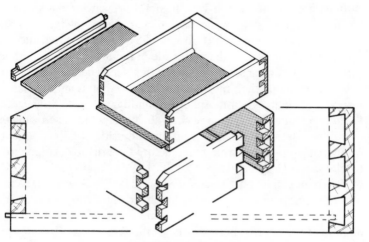

Fig. 6.53 A drawer

Methods of fixing table tops

Four methods by which table tops can be fixed to their frames are shown in Fig. 6.54.

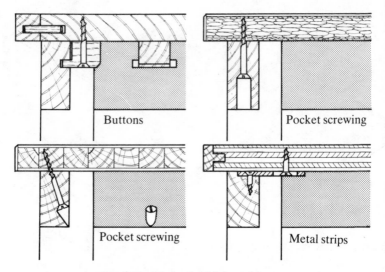

Fig. 6.54 Methods of fixing table tops

Buttons are purpose-made with lips and are sawn from strips of hardwood. Short, shallow mortises are cut around the inside of the rails to receive the lips of the buttons. The buttons are fitted into the mortises and screwed to the underside of the top. This is a method suitable for screwing solid wood tops in place. The button lips are able to slide along their mortises as the top expands and shrinks in response to changes in atmospheric humidity.

Pocket screwing Two types are shown. This method of screwing of tops down on to table frames from the underside of rails is suitable when fixing tops made from manufactured boards (e.g. chipboard, blockboard and plywood).

Metal strips can be purchased (see page 23). When screwed to the tops of the rails and also into the underside of the top, this is a very strong method of securing a top. They are suitable for both solid and manufactured boards, because one of the screw holes is slotted to allow movement of the screw along the slot.

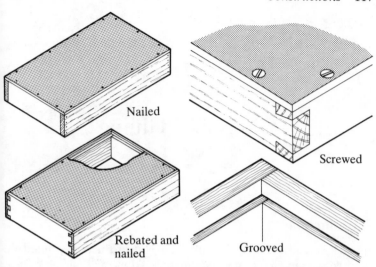

Fig. 6.55 Methods of fixing bottoms to boxes

Methods of fixing bottoms to boxes

The following four methods are illustrated in Fig. 6.55.

Nailed (and glued) bottoms are satisfactory, providing that the nails are not driven into the corners of the box frame. Driving in nails some 25 to 30 mm (1 in to 1¼ in) from the corners prevents the box sides splitting as the nails are hammered in.

Screwed bottoms can also be glued. Note again that the screws should be inserted clear of the box corners.

Rebated bottoms have rebates cut around the bottom edges of the box sides to receive the bottom. Jointing methods may have to be modified slightly to allow the rebates to be cleanly cut. Bottoms can be glued and nailed or screwed into the rebates.

Grooved bottoms have grooves cut around the lower insides of the box to allow the bottoms to be inserted. Bottoms fitted in this way have to be assembled in the grooves as the box itself is assembled. Gluing is not normally necessary.

7

Glues and Gluing

Introduction

If you first read and then carefully follow the instructions printed on their containers, modern wood glues are strong and reliable. They can be purchased from many shops in cans, tubes, plastic containers or packets, in small or large quantities, and as and when they are needed. The three glues of most value to woodworkers are pva, urea-formaldehyde and impact glues.

Polyvinyl acetate (pva) glues are the easiest of all modern adhesives to use. They can be purchased in ready-to-use plastic squeegee containers which are thrown away when empty. The adhesive is squeezed from the container directly on to the surfaces to be glued. The white, liquid glue sets chemically in about three or four hours

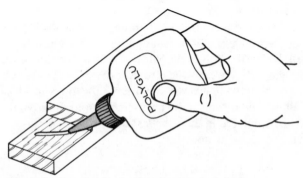

Fig. 7.1 Pva glue in plastic squeegee container

depending on room temperature. On warm days the glue sets more quickly than on cold days. Pva glue is sufficiently strong for all woodwork constructions, but as it is not waterproof, it is unsuitable for jointing parts of items of woodwork which may be subjected to damp. Joints made with pva glues need to be cramped or held together tightly until the glue sets. If the joints are screwed or nailed, cramping will of course be unnecessary. Examples of modern pva glues are 'Borden wood glue', 'Evostik wood glue', 'Croid polystik' among others.

Urea-formaldehyde glues make strong and water-resistant joints in woodwork. They are therefore suitable for work which might be exposed to damp. Two types can be purchased. The first is a white powder, of which 'Cascamite' is an example. The powder must be mixed with water to form a thick syrup before it can be applied. The second type is purchased in a two-part pack. An example of the second type is 'Aerolite'. This consists of a thick syrup and a liquid hardener. The two liquids must be mixed together before application, or the syrup applied to one part of a joint and the hardener to the other before the parts are joined together. Joints made with urea-formaldehyde adhesives must be kept under pressure while setting takes place. Setting is a chemical reaction known as polymerisation which occurs in about two hours in warm conditions, but takes longer in cold conditions.

Impact glues are rubber bases in solvents. They allow surfaces to adhere to each other directly they are placed together (i.e. on impact). They are of great value when gluing plastic laminates such as Formica sheet to wood, or for gluing fabrics to wood. They are not sufficiently strong for constructional jointing. The thick, paste-like adhesive is usually spread thinly over each of the surfaces of the parts to be glued together. You then wait for about fifteen minutes until the adhesive becomes tacky. The surfaces are then placed against each other and an instant bond is made. Some of these glues allow some movement after the surfaces are placed together. Examples of impact adhesives are Bostik and Titebond.

Three other glues which you may come across for joining wood to wood are Scotch glue, epoxy resin glue and hot-melt glue.

Scotch glues are made from animal bones and hides. They can be purchased ready-to-use ('Croid aero glue') or can be made from 'pearl' glue – small pieces of solid glue which need to be mixed with water and then heated to a liquid state. These glues are cheap and very strong, but not waterproof. Nor are they easy to use because they must be kept hot as they are applied and set as they chill.

Epoxy resin glues are not suitable for general woodwork as they are comparatively expensive. However, epoxy resins will hold together any materials: china, earthenware, metal, glass, most plastics. They are therefore of great value for occasions when other materials need to be joined to wood. The most common of this group is 'Araldite', which is sold in two-part packs of two tubes, each containing a thick resin. The two resins must be mixed together prior to application.

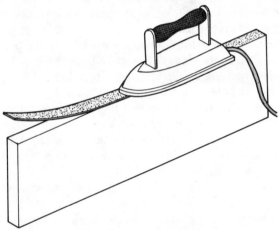

Fig. 7.2   Iron-on edging strip

Hot-melt glues are mentioned because iron-on edging veneer strips are coated with hot-melt glues on their rear surfaces. These glues are thermoplastic materials which melt when heated under the action of a hot iron and set firmly when cold. Hot-melt glues cannot normally be purchased from shops as can the other glues listed above.

Cramping

When pieces of wood are glued to each other, they usually need to be held tightly together until the glue sets. Parts to be glued can often be held tightly together with nails or screws while the adhesive sets. A bench vice makes a good cramping device for some work, if the vice is not required for other purposes at the time. A pile of books or other heavy articles will occasionally be sufficiently heavy to hold some parts, as for example when gluing claddings of ply or hardboard to a small door frame. Apart from these methods, the majority of cramping jobs can be carried out with bar (or sash) cramps or with G cramps.

When using such cramps, three basic rules should be observed. First, always use wooden cramping blocks between the work and the cramp jaws as the steel of the jaws can severely bruise the wood being placed under pressure. Second, the direction of the cramping must be set parallel to the parts along which pressure is being exerted. Third, always check that the work is square before putting it to one side while the glue hardens. Squareness can be checked either with the aid of a try square or, in those cases where rectangular frameworks are being cramped, by checking that the diagonals are equal in length.

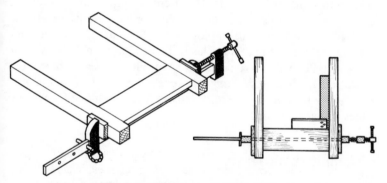

Fig. 7.3   Cramping with a bar cramp

Rules to observe when gluing

1   If the work is to be cramped, place the parts together in cramps before applying any glue. This is to check that the joints fit and the cramps have been adjusted to size. It is advisable to have a trial run of this kind so that any necessary alterations can be made.

2 The glue being used should be suitable for the purpose for which the work is being made.
3 Your hands, tools and bench should be clean, i.e. free from waste, tools, dust or shavings.
4 Mix only sufficient glue for the work to be glued.
5 Clean surplus glue off the work before it can set, with clean damp rags, or the corner of a chisel.
6 When synthetic resin glues have been used, wash your hands after the cramping is completed.
7 The adhesive can be applied from a squeegee container, by brush, or sometimes with a thin strip of wood, depending on the type of glue which is to be applied. If brushes are used with synthetic resin glues, they must be thoroughly washed after use, otherwise the glue will set hard and the brushes will be unsuitable for further work.

Other forms of cramping devices are available. There are a number of purpose-made spring clips for some forms of cramping. Some firms make frame cramps which consist of webbing or plastic cord with tightening devices. Handscrews, adjustable G cramps, corner mitre cramps and extension bars for bar cramps are among the tools you may wish to employ. Some forms of lightweight work can be held together with elastic bands, or with Sellotape or masking tape, which is removed when the glue has set. Some model work can be held together with veneer pins, driven home just sufficiently to hold the pieces tightly and then removed when the adhesive has hardened.

Cramping shaped frames

When assembling and gluing-up frames of an awkward shape, the addition of blocks of wood which have been glued to the frame members prior to their assembly can assist in secure and tight cramping. Figs 7.4 and 7.5 show examples of cramping with the aid of such blocks. With some work, gluing the shaped blocks to the frame parts may not be necessary as merely placing them between the frame and the cramps is sufficient. If blocks have been glued in place for cramping, they must be sawn and planed from the work after the glue has set.

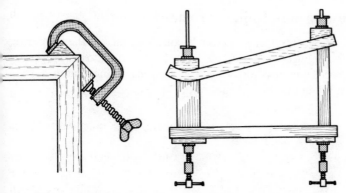

Fig. 7.4   Gluing and cramping awkwardly shaped frames

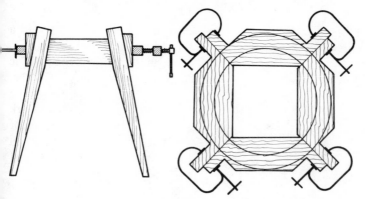

Fig. 7.5   Further examples of gluing and cramping awkward shapes

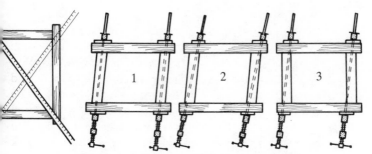

Fig. 7.6   Adjusting out-of-square frames

Adjusting out-of-square frames

Sometimes after applying cramps you may find that the framework you are gluing up is not square. Squareness can often be achieved on these occasions by adjusting the positions of the cramp bars, as illustrated in the three diagrams of Fig. 7.6.

8

Wood Finishing

Unprotected wooden surfaces are difficult to keep clean and can easily become damaged or dirty from handling, spillage of liquids, or other physical damage, such as resting hot plates on a table top. Stains, varnishes, polishes, oils and paints can all be applied to woods to provide protection or decoration. These 'finishes' protect woodwork against handling and make it easy to clean. Stains, varnishes and polishes will enhance grain and texture. Some finishes are resistant to heat and water and so are not damaged by water, or hot cups and plates. Wood in some situations, such as fencing, may also need protection against rotting and insects. There is a large variety of modern wood-finishing materials on sale which are normally quite easy to apply, but you should pay attention to the following two simple rules. First, you must always read the instructions and follow them as carefully as possible. Second, the surfaces to which the finish is to be applied must be smooth, clean and free from blemishes such as pencil marks, scratches, oil, dirt, dust or glue spots. A good quality polish or varnish properly applied will show up blemishes very clearly and make them even more unsightly than they were before the finish was applied. Time spent on the preparation of a wooden surface by removing tool marks, scratches, hammer marks, dents, torn grain, dirt and other faults, is amply repaid by the quality of the resulting surfaces after wood finishes have been applied. Good surfaces ready for the application of finishes can be obtained by sanding with sandpaper.

Sandpaper

Despite the free use of the term 'sanding', abrasive papers are no
made with sand as the abrading material. Four types of 'sandpaper'
are commonly available. These are: glasspaper, garnet paper
aluminium oxide paper and silicon carbide ('wet and dry') paper
Glasspaper is cheaper than the other types of 'sandpaper', but tend
to wear out more quickly. Aluminium oxide paper is very hardwear
ing and silicon carbide paper is principally designed for 'rubbing
down' old paintwork prior to re-painting. Garnet paper is a good
general-purpose sandpaper, but does not provide such a fine
smooth finish as glasspaper. Numerous grades of these abrasive
papers are made. The following table gives some indication of the
grades you are most likely to require:

	fine	*medium*	*coarse*
Glasspaper	1	1½	M2
Garnet paper	3/0	2/0	½
Aluminium oxide	120	100	60
Silicon carbide	120	100	60

Fig.8.1   Dividing a sheet of sandpaper into usable pieces

You can purchase coarser or finer grades than these if you need
them. Sandpapers are usually purchased in sheets each measuring
about 280 mm by 230 mm (11 in by 9 in) which can be cut into six

pieces for sanding purposes. This can be done by tearing against a strip of wood. Small packets of sandpaper cut ready to size for immediate use can be purchased in many shops.

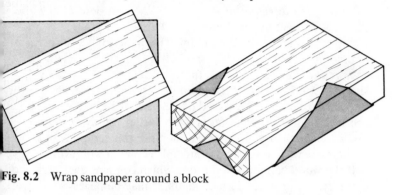

Fig. 8.2 Wrap sandpaper around a block

When sanding a surface, wrap the sandpaper around a block of wood or around a purpose-made cork glasspaper block. This not only helps to keep the surface you are smoothing truly flat, but also prevents the sandpaper from wearing out quickly. An old saying that 'sandpaper is the most expensive tool in the workshop' rings even more true if it is wasted by adopting careless methods of working. Firmer pressure can also be applied if the paper is wrapped around a block. Ensure the piece of wood being worked is securely held, either by cramping, or in a vice, if it is not large or heavy enough to be worked without it moving.

Another abrasive material you will find to be of value when needing to smooth hard polished or varnished surfaces, is fine steel wool. This material is used in wads, without the aid of a block.

A sixth type of prepared abrasive material you may come across is tungsten carbide grit mounted on flexible metal sheets. This is made in blocks especially designed to hold the sheets and is useful when removing old paint or old polish from wood. It is not a suitable sheet to use when preparing surfaces before applying a 'finish'.

Sanding wood

To obtain a good surface before the application of any wood finish, first plane the wood as smooth as possible. Then wrap a piece of coarse glasspaper, for example, grade M2, or garnet paper, say grade ½, around a sandpaper block and pressing firmly downwards with the hands, work the sandpaper all over the surface *always following the direction of the grain*. When all defects have been removed, repeat the operation, but with a finer grade, say grade 1 glasspaper or grade 100 aluminium oxide paper. It may be necessary with some very hard woods to sand a third time with a yet finer grade of abrasive paper. Sand with the grain, and the scratches will not show. If you sand across the grain, the resulting scratches are very difficult to remove. This sanding, in two or three stages, should produce smooth clean surfaces ready for any finish. If this process takes longer than you expect, remember this time has been well spent if you wish to see a first-rate finish on your woodwork.

If the wood being worked is one which contains deep scratches, grain 'tears', or other surface faults, it may be necessary to work over the surfaces to be finished with a cabinet scraper; after planing, but before sanding. Details of cabinet scrapers and how to sharpen them are given on page 54. If bruising, for instance by hammer blows, is present on a wood surface to be prepared for finishing, dampening of the surface with water may 'raise the grain' sufficiently to swell out the bruises. Steaming with a wet rag and a hot iron will swell out even a deep bruise.

Wood finishes

Wood finishes include: stains, french polishes, polyurethane varnishes, polyester lacquers, cellulose lacquers, oils, waxes, paints, creosotes and various preservative finishes. Short descriptions of these various finishes are given below.

Stains

You may find some of your woodwork needs to be stained if you wish to match the colour of some existing woodwork. However, it is probably best to avoid staining if possible as most woods look best with a 'natural' finish which allows the original colours of the wood to be seen to full advantage. If staining is necessary, the unskilled person would be advised to purchase ready-made, oil-based stains, which are sold in cans of convenient sizes ready for immediate application. These can be applied with a brush or with clean rag.

After staining, a polish, lacquer, or other finish will normally be required.

French polish

French polishes are shellacs dissolved in methylated spirits with the addition of hardening gums. Some modern french polishes are thin polyurethane lacquers. To achieve a full french polish finish requires some practice and skill, but french polish is a very good wood sealer for the less experienced. A pleasing soft sheen can be obtained by applying two or three coats of white french polish with a brush, allowing them to dry, then lightly sanding to a very smooth surface with grade 0 glasspaper. This seals the wood, which can then be polished with a wax polish.

A full, hard-wearing wood finish using polyurethane french polish can be achieved by the following method:

1. Apply a brush coat of clear polyurethane varnish which has been thinned with an equal amount of white spirit. Allow to dry.
2. Apply a second brush coat of unthinned polyurethane varnish. Allow to dry.
3. Smooth with a fine garnet paper (grade 9/0).
4. Make up a polishing 'rubber' of cottonwool and fine rag (old handkerchieves are ideal). Charge the cottonwool with polyurethane french polish and cover with the rag. Working with a sweeping circular movement, apply some ten or so coats of the polish, re-charging the cottonwool with polish as the rubber dries out.
5. Allow to dry and smooth with grade 9/0 garnet paper.
6. Apply a second series of about ten coats of polish with the rubber, until a good body of polish has been built up.
7. Allow to dry and smooth with grade 9/0 garnet paper.
8. Apply a few thinned coats of the polish, working only along the grain of the wood, and allow to dry.
9. Burnish the dry, hard polished surface along the grain with a dry, clean duster.
10. The resulting brilliant polish can be 'dulled' by dusting pumice powder on to the polish and working over the surface with a soft clothes brush. The pumice slightly abrades the brilliance to a matt finish; a french polish which some people prefer to a brilliant finish.

Polyurethane varnishes

Clear polyurethane varnish applied in two brush coats, with a drying interval between, will produce an excellent finish. If the second coat is allowed to harden completely for six or seven days and then lightly rubbed along the grain with fine wire wool, the resulting sheen is very pleasing. Afterwards the surface must be thoroughly cleaned with a duster to remove all traces of the wire wool. Polyurethane varnish finishes are sufficiently heatproof to resist boiling water without damage. Tinted polyurethane varnishes produce pleasing coloured finishes, through which the wood grain can be seen. Polyurethane varnishes which produce matt finishes can also be purchased.

Polyester lacquers

Polyester lacquers are acid-catalysed lacquers supplied in two packs which must be mixed together just prior to application – a coating and a hardener. The hardener is added to the lacquer according to the directions printed on the container holding the two liquids. Such acid-catalysed lacquers produce an extremely clear finish with minimal colour staining of the underlying wood. The resulting finish will resist staining by hot water or by hot crockery. Coloured varieties can be obtained in addition to the clear lacquers. Apply by brush or by spray gun.

Cellulose lacquers

A quick-drying lacquer formed by dissolving cellulose in 'thinners' can be applied by spray gun and is available either clear or in a range of colours. If applied by brush, it is advisable to apply several coats of the lacquer thinned about 50/50 with cellulose thinners, in place of a single full strength coat. As a wood sealer, prior to wax polishing, several brush coats of thinned cellulose lacquer form an excellent base for wax polishing.

Oils

Teak oil, on sale in many shops, is an excellent finish for all dark-coloured woods. It should be applied with a soft rag in two coats, with an interval of a day or so between. The resulting oiled surface is matt and smooth, displaying a dull sheen which suits woods with a dark colour, such as teak, iroko or afrormosia. Linseed oil can be rubbed into wood to give an oiled finish, but it takes several weeks to dry. Thin coats of linseed oil rubbed on hardwoods at weekly intervals over a period of several months produces a pleasing light gold coloured and hard-wearing sheen. Olive oil is a suitable finish for wooden items made for containing food, such as fruit bowls.

Wax polishes

Floor and furniture wax polishes will provide excellent, easily-applied wood finishes. A sealer is necessary to prevent the wax sinking into the wood. French polish, thin, clear cellulose lacquer and polyurethane varnish thinned with white spirit are all good sealers for this purpose. The wax should be applied and then burnished with clean rags or dusters.

Paints

Softwoods such as pines and redwood can be painted without difficulty providing the surfaces are clean and smooth, using either a primer coat followed by an undercoat, followed by a top coat (gloss) or two coats of a polyurethane paint. Hardwood, however, will need to be 'filled in' before it can be painted, otherwise the paint will sink into the open cells of the hardwood surfaces. Such fillings can consist of a thin paste of Polyfilla or plaster of Paris, rubbed in with a coarse rag and sanded when quite dry. Proprietary brands of wood fillers may also be found to be suitable for filling-in the grain of hardwoods before painting.

Creosote

Two brush coats of creosote will protect fencing, sheds, gate posts and other outdoor woodwork against rotting and insects. Further brush coats are advisable every second year. Other preservative liquids are available for this purpose and some of the proprietary brands are easy to apply and free from the dangers inherent with the application of creosote, such as the damage which can occur if it comes into contact with the skin of anyone prone to skin irritation.

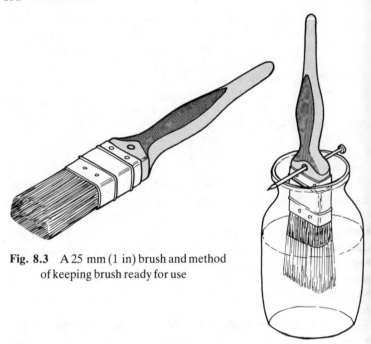

Fig. 8.3   A 25 mm (1 in) brush and method
of keeping brush ready for use

Cleaning brushes

Brushes must be cleaned after being used to apply wood finishes.
The fluid most frequently used is white spirit (turps substitute),
although methylated spirits should be used for cleaning brushes
which have applied french polish, and cellulose thinners for those
which have applied cellulose lacquer. After cleaning in these liquids, all brushes should be thoroughly washed with hot water and
soap, and then placed to one side to dry out. In between coats,
brushes can be suspended in a tin or jar of the appropriate liquid.

9

Safety

Some rules for taking safety precautions have already been given in Chapter 4 and are repeated in this chapter. The importance of safe working cannot be over-emphasised. An understanding of the importance of taking sensible safety precautions and the use of safe procedures when manipulating tools and machines is essential. It is better to be safe than sorry as a lost finger or a lost hand cannot be replaced. Accidents should not occur when working with tools and, if sensible safety precautions are taken, accidents will not occur. The rules for prevention of accidents in workshop conditions may be summarised by three guidelines:

Observe a regular routine of maintenance.
Use your common sense.
Wear the correct clothing.

The workshop and hand tools

A regular routine of maintenance of tools and equipment is essential for safe working. Tools should be maintained in a sharp, clean and correctly adjusted condition. Blunt, dirty or wrongly adjusted tools may lead to accidents because the tools do not act as expected by the user and may slip and cut the person rather than the material being worked. A blunt gouge, for example, can slip, and literally 'gouge' flesh from the person using it. Shavings and scraps of wood should not be left to accumulate on the floor, as people may slip on them as they move about. Nor should shavings and scraps be allowed to accumulate on bench tops, as they can cause tools to fall off, which may cause accidents or lead to doubt over how work can be suitably positioned on the bench. Similarly, odd lengths of wood should not be allowed to accumulate. They should be re-stored or, if too small, disposed of in a waste bin.

Bench tops should be kept as clear as possible of tools and pieces of material. Regular attention to this detail prevents those accidents which can occur when sharp tools are knocked off bench tops and cut legs and feet. Regular attention should be given to the tightness and general condition of tool handles. Handles should always be firmly set on tools, and the screws on saw and plane handles should be secure. Handles should be clean and free from splits or other damage, as loose or damaged handles may cause a tool to react in an unexpected way.

Common sense is essential in the use of any workshop. Walk with care; do not run from place to place. Boards should be carried with respect for others in a workshop. A long board slipping or swinging could lead to serious accidents. Tools must also be carried in a manner which does not allow others to be damaged by them. 'Sharp edges down' is a good rule to observe when carrying tools from place to place. Before any work starts on second-hand wood, ensure that all nails and other pieces of metal are removed, as these may damage cutting edges of saw, plane or chisel. Once again, damaged or blunted cutting edges, caused by striking a nail, say, can be the cause of an accident.

Attention should be paid to personal clothing if accidents are to be avoided. It is advisable to wear a carpenter's apron, which presents a smooth front to work and equipment, or to wear overalls of some kind. These prevent ties, pockets and flapping coats from catching and upsetting tools and equipment. If working in shirt sleeves, roll them tightly on the arms to prevent the cuffs catching on your work or the sleeves slipping down at an unexpected moment. Long hair can be a nuisance in a workshop and should be restrained by suitable headgear. Strong shoes or boots are advisable to prevent damage to feet and toes if tools or equipment fall on them.

Tools should be racked or stored in boxes, cupboards or drawers with a specific place for each tool. This racking helps to ensure that each tool is stored in a suitable manner and also means that you will know exactly where to find each tool as it is required. Racks should be designed so that anyone taking a tool from its rack is not damaged by the cutting edge of other tools.

Lighting in a workshop is of great importance. It is never safe to work under lighting conditions in which the work and tools cannot be seen quite clearly. The more natural light – from window, sky light, roof or doorway – the better, but if artificial light is needed, see that it is adequate and positioned for maximum effect.

No matter how small your workshop or working area may be, you will need to store some materials which are potentially dangerous. Some finishes such as paints, varnishes, polishes and lacquers are combustible, and due attention should be given to this when selecting storage places for them. With the increased use of aerosol spray cans, remember these should only be stored in cool conditions and not in any place in direct sunlight. A waste bin of some kind is advisable for the disposal of unwanted scraps, shavings and other waste. Waste bins should be emptied daily.

When using synthetic resin glues and some types of finishing materials, such as creosote and some oil stains, wash your hands when the task is finished as some such materials can cause skin irritation. Personally, I would never saw, drill or otherwise cut any form of asbestos sheeting, as the dust which arises from such sheeting can be extremely dangerous. When working chipboards and some woods which give rise to dusts which affect the respiratory system, it is advisable to wear some form of filter type face mask. The irritation caused to the respiratory system by such dusts can be quite severe. When painting work such as children's toys, select the paint with due regard to the fact that such work may be sucked or licked by the child playing with it. Some paints can be dangerous, so seek advice from the manufacturer if you are at all unsure of the safety of the finish.

Machine tools

Any power tool should be maintained in a good condition. It should be kept dry and clean and its cutters should be sharpened regularly. If there are any doubts about its electrical insulation, the machine should be inspected and, if necessary, repaired by a competent electrician. The cable connecting a power tool to its source of supply must be maintained in a good condition, not damaged or frayed. A damaged cable or bad plug connection can be a source of danger both to the person operating the tool and to others nearby. Before connecting a plug to an electric outlet socket, the job for which the tool is required should be made ready and the plug inserted into the socket only when the power tool is required. Tools or attachments should be securely fitted to the tool before inserting the plug and any subsequent changes or adjustments must not be made until the switch at the outlet socket is in its OFF position.

When a hand power tool is being operated, particular attention should be given to the position of the cable. The cable must not be positioned so that tools or equipment can be upset or where people, including the operator, can be tripped. The cord must not be kinked, as this can break or damage the leads inside the cable insulation, and it is advisable not to allow the lead to trail in water, such as in a puddle when working in the open air. When using a power tool care must be taken to avoid any possibility of the cable being cut by the power tool's cutting action.

You should keep your hands dry, and where appropriate, goggles and/or masks should be worn. In particular, a sensible precaution is to wear a respiratory mask of the filter type when using sandpapering devices. Also, as has already been noted, some woods and all chipboards give off dusts which can be harmful when worked by machines. Thus when sawing, drilling, planing or sanding such materials with the aid of power tools, a filter mask should be regarded as a 'must'. The operator should ensure that his stance is such that he cannot be easily thrown off balance. Work should be held quite securely – in a vice, by cramps or by other holding devices – unless it is heavy enough to prevent movement as it is being worked. Both hands should be used on hand power tools as often as possible. Try to prevent spectators standing around when anybody is working with power tools, as they may distract the operator from the concentration necessary when working with such tools.

Modern machine tools are provided with suitable guards. These guards should always be in place and properly adjusted when the tools are operating. Some guards are designed to prevent actual physical contact between the operator and the cutting edges, for example, circular saw guards. Some are designed to guard moving parts such as belts and pulleys and others are designed to prevent chips and dust flying from the work hitting the face, and in particular the eyes, of the operator. This type of guard is often made from clear acrylic sheet which can become dirty and almost opaque as a result. Therefore make sure that plastic guards which have to be transparent, are kept clean. When using machine tools such as grinding machines, always wear goggles. It may also be advisable to wear goggles when working on any machine from which chips, shavings or dust are being thrown off as the tool cuts. The wood being worked should be held securely in the machine, i.e. screwed tightly to faceplates on lathes, held firmly in cramps on a mortising machine, or otherwise firmly 'chucked' or cramped. When using a machine grinder wheel of the carborundum type, ensure that the tool post is placed as close to the rotating wheel as possible, to avoid the work being ground from slipping down between rest and wheel. Never apply undue pressure on such grinding wheels. They have been known to explode under unnecessarily heavy pressure.

10

Woodwork Design

Before you start making anything from wood, plan its design. Nothing can be so disappointing when woodworking as to spend a great deal of time, energy and money in making a piece of work only to find that the result looks wrong, or is not going to work properly. A good policy when designing is to set your ideas down on paper first. A few freehand sketches, developed as ideas grow, can be the basis for proper working drawings of a final design. With very simple projects, such preliminaries may not be needed, but with projects of any complexity, this policy pays good dividends. If all the details of a design are first drawn or written down on paper, answers to any problems can be discovered before tools are put to wood.

The drawing of sketches which are the groundwork to a final design need not be time-consuming, but the potential designer does need to develop some draughtsmanship skills. These are: to be able to make simple freehand sketches and to produce drawings with drawing instruments. Freehand sketches need not be full of technical details, but they should be attempted in good proportions to enable the designer to see, on paper, if his ideas 'look right'. The somewhat tedious exercise of committing ideas to paper inevitably saves time and money as problems can be solved on paper rather than by wasting expensive timber. Even the crudest drawings and simplest notes are better than nothing.

Notes and sketches

Start by writing notes on a large piece of paper. Resist the temptation to scribble, and list your ideas neatly in columns. It is far easier to check back on a well laid out list than to fumble through random scribblings. Add sketches to show in picture form the ideas you have written in your notes. These notes and sketches could follow a laid down sequence like the following:

1 Main requirements and sizes

What is required of the design? What essential dimensions need to be considered? Check with a ruler on existing pieces of work e.g. for furniture, garden apparatus, buildings, doors etc. Check with a ruler the size of a human being in relation to the piece; when seated, standing, writing, eating, working space required etc. If the design is connected with storage, for example bookshelves, sewing equipment, cutlery, crockery etc., check the sizes of the items to be stored. When designing, a golden rule is always to use a rule and keep on measuring until you are quite certain that the sizes chosen are suited to the design you wish to make.

2 Proportions

Does the design look well proportioned? If it has been ergonomically well designed – that is to suit human needs – then the proportions will probably look good. Don't however be fully content with accepting this rule of thumb. Not only are the overall proportions of importance, but so are the proportions of its parts. Are the legs too thick or too thin, are the thicknesses and widths of rails well proportioned, are the drawers too wide, are the doors well proportioned etc.? Do such minor proportions look right?

3 Shape and form

Basically all constructional woodwork can be divided into three forms: flat frames, three-dimensional frames and boxes. These three forms must be borne in mind when designing items of woodwork. Other details of shape will also need considering, such as tapers, curves, mouldings, turnings and carved parts. Each of these details must be considered in relation to the overall shape and form. Often minor shapes such as mouldings and curves may be unnecessarily complex and often can be left out altogether, but on the other hand, a well designed curve can enhance a whole design.

4   **Materials**
Which woods do you wish to use? Are they suitable in colour, grain, figure, weight, flexibility and strength? Are they readily available? If not, will others do equally well? An appendix on page 179 lists a number of woods and gives their suitability for certain purposes. Much of the work which you will be attempting can well be carried out in any of a variety of available woods. However, if a design is to be successful, careful consideration must be given to the choice of woods. Other materials will also have to be considered, such as manufactured boards, laminated plastic, upholstery materials, any metals used in conjunction with woods, glass, mirrors and any other materials which a design may require.

5   **Construction**
With the advent of the new modern constructional methods, many designs can now be made with comparative ease, that were not possible using traditional methods. The two most important modern methods are the increasing use of manufactured boards and the availability of 'Knock-Down' jointings (see page 100). However, the traditional constructional methods must still be considered in relation to many woodwork designs. The methods chosen will depend partly on the skill of the person who is making the design, for example, should the method be simple or complex? The best adhesive should also be considered when deciding on the kind of construction. A selection of suitable constructional methods can be made from those shown in Chapter 6.

6   **Fittings**
List all the fittings required – screws, nails, hinges, catches, handles, and so on. You will then avoid the frustration of getting to a stage in making a design when a pair of hinges, say, is required and you have not got the correct size to hand. In listing the fittings you will need, you should consider the material and the quality of the fittings required by the design. For example, good quality brass hinges and screws might be considered necessary when designing a piece of furniture, whereas steel hinges and steel screws would be considered suitable for a dining-room hatch door.

7 Costs

Write a cutting list of all the materials required and put down the cost against each item. Include the costs of any necessary fittings and do not forget items such as the adhesives required. You may well find that the overall costs of the planned design are too high and that economies will need to be made. You may even find the costs to be less than anticipated, in which case better, more expensive fittings, for example, may be included. Be careful that unnecessary economies do not spoil your design. The work you will be putting into the item will probably be worth considerably more than all the materials and fittings involved.

8 Surface finish

The finish to be applied to your design must be chosen with care. Should it be resistant to heat or water? Does it need to be weatherproof? Is a colour required, or is it best to leave it as 'natural' wood colour? Must the finish be tough to withstand a great deal of handling? The answers to these and other such questions will determine the choice of finish you will apply.

9 Special factors

Many factors other than those given above may need consideration. One particular factor may be safety. Are all the corners and edges of the design finished in such a manner that they will not cut, bruise or damage those using it? If you are making toys, is the applied finish safe for children to handle, and even to put in their mouths? Are you using materials which may present a fire hazard (some polyurethane foam upholstery materials should be avoided)? Is the weight of the design an important factor? Are you including glass or mirrors in the design? Will parts of your design need to be sealed against weather, as, for example, when fitting a roof, a window or a door? All such special factors relating to your design should be fully considered and, if possible, all their requirements should be fully satisfied.

10 Working drawing

By the time you have noted and drawn the details relating to the considerations given above, you will have a clear idea of the final design. A good working drawing should now be made, although it is not absolutely essential. Whilst making this drawing you may well come across further details which need amendment. Remember, it is far better to solve such problems on paper than to spoil materials later. The usual method of producing a working drawing is with the aid of drawing instruments, i.e. Tee square, set square, ruler protractor, compasses and pencils. Front views, end views and plans, together with sectional views showing cuts taken through interior parts, are usually incorporated in a working drawing. One important detail is the inclusion of all dimensions. The aim in making a working drawing should be that the design can be made completely from the drawing without having to seek information elsewhere.

Examples of designing

Two examples are given in the following pages of the method of designing outlined above. These are both items of furniture; one a comparatively simple construction which many woodworkers will be asked to undertake – a coffee table. The second is a more complex construction – a needlework cabinet.

Completion of design analysis of needlework cabinet

In the drawings on pages 146, 147 and 148, the analysis for the design of a needlework cabinet deals with the requirements of the design, giving its dimensions, proportions, shape and form, materials, method of construction and a working drawing. To complete the analysis, a list of fittings, a cutting list, the proposed surface finish and any special factors arising, will be considered.

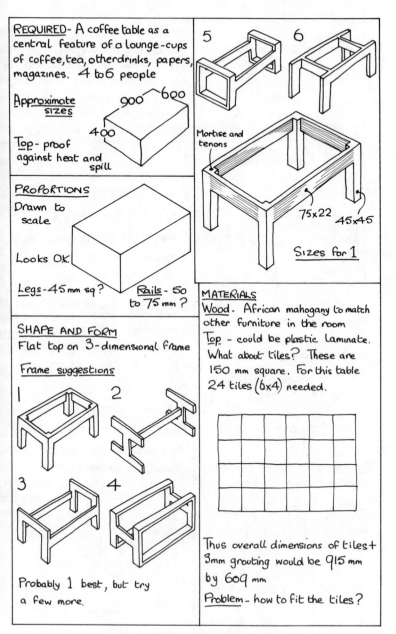

REQUIRED - A coffee table as a central feature of a lounge - cups of coffee, tea, other drinks, papers, magazines. 4 to 6 people

Approximate sizes

900   600
400

Top - proof against heat and spill

PROPORTIONS
Drawn to scale

Looks O.K.

Legs - 45 mm sq?   Rails - 50 to 75 mm?

SHAPE AND FORM
Flat top on 3-dimensional frame

Frame suggestions

1   2
3   4

Probably 1 best, but try a few more.

5   6

Mortise and tenons

75×22   45×45

Sizes for 1

MATERIALS
Wood. African mahogany to match other furniture in the room

Top - could be plastic laminate. What about tiles? These are 150 mm square. For this table 24 tiles (6×4) needed.

Thus overall dimensions of tiles + 3mm grouting would be 915 mm by 609 mm

Problem - how to fit the tiles?

Fig. 10.1   Coffee table: design sheet 1

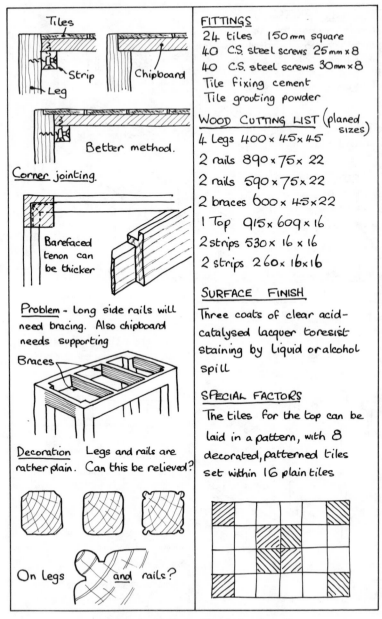

Tiles

Strip

Leg

Chipboard

Better method.

Corner jointing.

Barefaced tenon can be thicker

Problem - Long side rails will need bracing. Also chipboard needs supporting

Braces

Decoration   Legs and rails are rather plain. Can this be relieved?

On legs and rails?

FITTINGS
24 tiles   150 mm square
40 C.S. steel screws 25 mm × 8
40 C.S. steel screws 30 mm × 8
Tile fixing cement
Tile grouting powder

WOOD CUTTING LIST (planed sizes)
4 Legs 400 × 45 × 45
2 rails 890 × 75 × 22
2 rails 590 × 75 × 22
2 braces 600 × 45 × 22
1 Top 915 × 609 × 16
2 strips 530 × 16 × 16
2 strips 260 × 16 × 16

SURFACE FINISH
Three coats of clear acid-catalysed lacquer to resist staining by liquid or alcohol spill

SPECIAL FACTORS
The tiles for the top can be laid in a pattern, with 8 decorated, patterned tiles set within 16 plain tiles

Fig. 10.2   Coffee table: design sheet 2

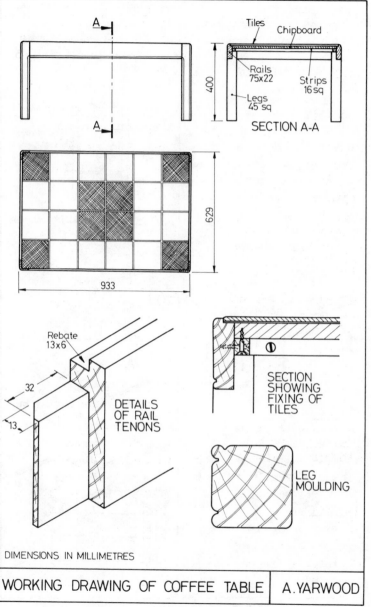

A

Tiles　Chipboard

SECTION A-A

Rails
75×22

Strips
16 sq

Legs
45 sq

400

629

933

Rebate
13×6

32

13

DETAILS
OF RAIL
TENONS

SECTION
SHOWING
FIXING OF
TILES

LEG
MOULDING

DIMENSIONS IN MILLIMETRES

WORKING DRAWING OF COFFEE TABLE | A.YARWOOD

Fig. 10.3　Coffee table: design sheet 3

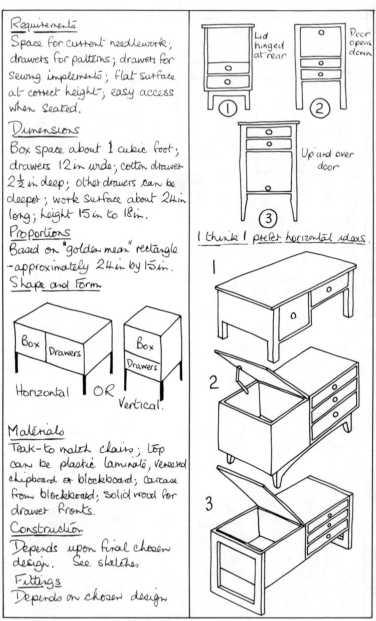

Requirements

Space for current needlework; drawers for patterns; drawers for sewing implements; flat surface at correct height; easy access when seated.

Dimensions

Box space about 1 cubic foot; drawers 12 in wide; cotton drawer 2½ in deep; other drawers can be deeper; work surface about 24 in long; height 15 in to 18 in.

Proportions

Based on "golden mean" rectangle - approximately 24 in by 15 in.

Shape and Form

Box | Drawers

Horizontal OR Vertical.

Box | Drawers

Materials

Teak- to match chairs; top can be plastic laminate, veneered chipboard or blockboard; carcase from blockboard; solid wood for drawer fronts.

Construction

Depends upon final chosen design. See sketches

Fittings

Depends on chosen design

① Lid hinged at rear

② Door opens down

③ Up and over door

I think I prefer horizontal ideas.

Fig. 10.4 Needlework cabinet: design sheet 1

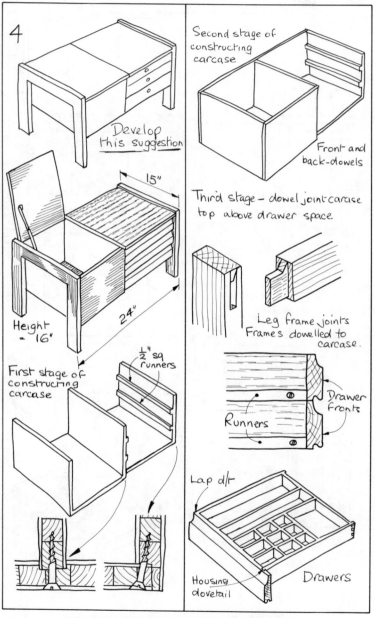

4

Develop this suggestion

15"

Height - 16"

24"

First stage of constructing carcase

½" sq runners

Second stage of constructing carcase

Front and back-dowels

Third stage — dowel joint carase top above drawer space

Leg frame joints
Frames dowelled to carcase.

Runners

Drawer Fronts

Lap d/t

Housing dovetail

Drawers

Fig. 10.5 Needlework cabinet: design sheet 2

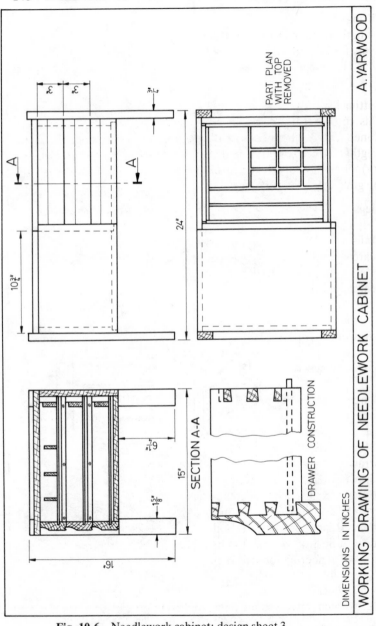

Fig. 10.6   Needlework cabinet: design sheet 3

Fittings

1 length nylon piano hinge 10¾ in long
1 stay for box lid
12 × 1½ in gauge 8 screws
12 × 1 in gauge 6 screws

Cutting list

This cutting list is a sawing list showing sizes before material is planed to size. The following allowances have been made: ½ inch to lengths, ¼ inch to widths and ⅛ inch to thicknesses (where necessary). Note that length is measured *along* the grain and width *across* the grain.

4 legs	17 in by 1⅞ in by ⅞ in (allow 1 in to length for 'horn')
2 rails	14½ in by 1⅞ in by ⅞ in
1 carcase end	10⅜ in by 13¼ in by ⅝ in veneered blockboard
1 carcase partition	10 in by 13¼ in by ⅝ in blockboard
1 carcase end	10⅜ in by 14⅝ in by ⅝ in veneered blockboard
1 drawer carcase top	12¼ in by 15¼ in by ⅝ in plastic laminate veneered blockboard
1 carcase back	23 in by 10⅜ in by ⅝ in veneered blockboard
1 carcase bottom	22¼ in by 14⅝ in by ⅝ in blockboard
1 box lid	11¼ in by 15¼ in by ⅝ in plastic laminate veneered blockboard
6 drawer runners	14⅞ in by ¾ in by ⅝ in
3 drawer fronts	12¼ in by 3¼ in by ⅞ in
6 drawer sides	13½ in by 2¾ in by ½ in
3 drawer backs	11⅝ in by 2 in by ½ in
3 drawer bottoms	14 in by 11¼ in by 3 mm plywood
2 drawer partitions	12½ in by 2 in by ⅜ in
5 drawer partitions	7 in by 2 in by ⅜ in

Strips of veneering for visible edges of blockboard

Surface finish

Clear french polyurethane polish dulled to semi matt.

No special factors arise.

11

Workshop Practice

As an example of some of the workshop practices involved in making items of woodwork, a detailed explanation of how to make the tiled coffee table described on pages 143–5 is now given. This explanation follows a sequence of procedures which is commonly involved in making pieces of woodwork under workshop conditions. Different procedures will be required in other forms of woodwork, such as the construction of a fence, the building of a garden shed, or the putting up of a shelf. The workshop procedures necessary for making the tiled coffee table follow this sequence: preparing material to size; marking and numbering the parts for assembly; marking out of joints; cutting of joints; assembling the construction; any further procedures necessary before the construction can finally be assembled; gluing and cramping; cleaning up ready for the application of surface finish and applying the surface finish.

Preparing material to size

If you wish to make furniture of a good quality, it is necessary to hand plane the pieces of wood making up its parts before beginning the construction. Each piece of a good quality item of woodwork needs to be straight and square and accurately planed to its correct finished size. Machine planed timber is quite satisfactory for some of the work attempted by woodworkers; for example, if you are laying floorboards, or cladding a wall with match boarding, or making the frame for a workshop in the garden, then hand planing of the wood is not necessary. However, for most bench work, particularly when making furniture and many fittings for indoors, hand planing is almost essential. Without careful preparation of each piece of wood, your finished work cannot be accurately assembled and will never 'look right'. Parts which are not straight or square cannot be altered once a piece of work has been finally assembled.

If each part is to be hand planed, it is usual to allow 6 mm (¼ in) extra width and 3 mm (⅛ in) extra thickness on each piece being prepared, to allow for planing waste. A definite procedure should be followed to achieve a good degree of accuracy. The most common procedure is as follows (see Fig. 11.1):

1 Plane one side, which is then known as the face side. Check its straightness and flatness and mark it as the face side.
2 Plane one edge, which is known as the face edge. Check that it is straight, and also square to the face side, then mark it as the face edge.
3 Set a marking gauge to the required finished width. Mark the width with the gauge along the face side, measuring from the face edge.
4 Plane to the gauge line, checking the edge as it is planed for squareness with the face side.
5 Set a marking gauge to the required thickness. Mark this thickness along both edges, measuring from the face side.

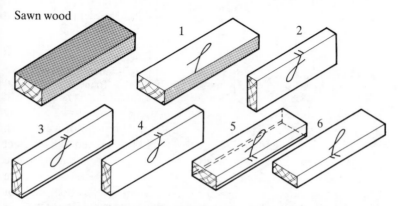

Fig. 11.1 Stages in preparing wood to size by hand planing

6   Plane to these gauge lines, checking the side being planed for flatness.

Saw, and if necessary plane, all pieces to their required lengths.

Marking ready for assembly

Before attempting any of the required constructional features, mark and number all parts in relation to each other. Follow a set routine when positioning face side and face edge marks. Three examples of such positioning of face marks are shown in Fig. 11.2, which includes numbering of the parts for the tiled table frame. Always mark each piece of each constructional feature with numbers.

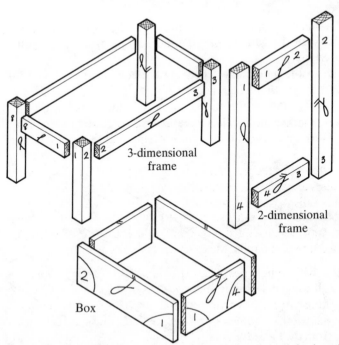

Fig. 11.2   Examples of face side and edge marks and numbering of parts

Marking out of joints

Now the marking out of individual joints can commence. The best procedure is to mark out as much as is possible of all the joint details for all parts of the work at one session. This saves time because the marking tools do not then need resetting. This procedure is also probably more accurate as it avoids errors creeping in, which is possible if several sessions of marking occur. For the tiled table frame the marking procedure would be:

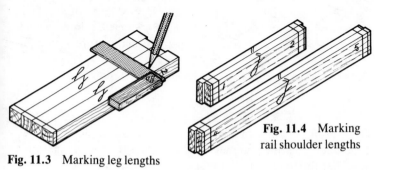

Fig. 11.4 Marking rail shoulder lengths

Fig. 11.3 Marking leg lengths

1 Cramp together all four legs or hold them together in a bench vice. Mark on to them their overall length and the positions of the rails.
2 Cramp together the two short rails and mark on them the tenon shoulders and overall lengths. Repeat with the long rails.
3 Saw the rails to their finished length.
4 Set the points of a mortise gauge to the thickness of a 13 mm (½ in) mortise chisel. Set the points at the correct distance from the face side of the rails. Mark all tenons and all mortises.

Note that with some types of construction it will not be possible to complete all joint marking in one session. An example would be when marking carcases involving dovetail joints. The usual method of making dovetails is to mark and cut the 'tails' and then to mark the 'pins' from the already cut tails. Even here, however, as much of the marking out as possible should be carried out in one session.

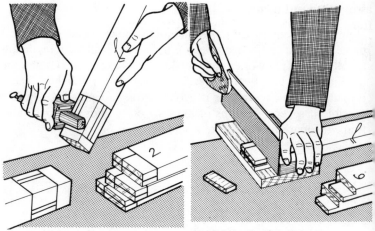

Fig. 11.5 Marking mortises **Fig. 11.6** Sawing tenons

Cutting joints

Once again, adopt a method by which all sawing, for example, is completed, before commencing another set of tool operations. Whether the tenons on the rails of the table frame should be sawn before the mortises in the legs are chopped or vice versa is a matter of personal choice. If you choose to shape the tenons first, then saw all of them before picking up mallet and chisel for the chopping of the mortises. Even in the sawing process, it will be quicker to saw all the down grain cuts before sawing all the across grain cuts. In the example of the tiled table, do not forget that grooves will need to be sawn and chiselled inside the leg rails to receive the two bracing rails which reinforce the chipboard for the top.

Checking the construction

When all the jointing is completed, try assembling the entire construction. Do not be tempted to check each joint as it is completed. If any of the joints require correction – by chiselling, sawing or planing to ensure a good fit between meeting parts – now is the time to make such adjustments. It is even advisable at this stage to cramp parts together to ensure that they go completely home. Thus, first check that the two end frames of the table can be assembled, and then check that the long rails will fit into the end frames to complete the whole of the table frame. When you are sure that all the mortise and tenons joining the rails to the legs are a good fit, check the fit of the two bracing rails.

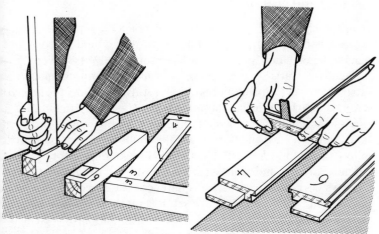

Fig. 11.7   Checking constructions   **Fig. 11.8**   Shaping bead moulding
with a scratch stock

Further procedures

When satisfied that all the necessary jointing is complete and that the construction can be assembled without difficulty, check which further operations are required before the work can be finally glued together. Two details will now need attention when making the tiled table. Rebates will need to be cut along the upper edges on the insides of all rails to receive the tiles, and the mouldings along the lower edges on the outside of the rails and on the legs will have to be shaped. The rebates can be cut with a rebate plane. The mouldings could be shaped with the aid of a scratch stock. The leg mouldings can only be partially cut at this stage as the final shaping of these in the corners where the rail mouldings join the leg mouldings must be left until after the frames have been glued together. Another procedure which must be followed at this stage is to clean up all inner surfaces thoroughly, by scraping and sanding, or by fine planing and sanding. All those parts which cannot be easily cleaned up after the assembly has been glued, should be cleaned up at this stage.

Gluing and cramping

Always check that an assembly will cramp together accurately square before applying any glue. If work is found to be out-of-square when glued, or if the work cannot be fully assembled, great difficulty can arise in attempting to achieve squareness and correct assembly. Always place pieces of waste softwood under the heads of cramps to avoid bruising the wood being cramped. Frames such as the tiled table frame will need to be glued in two stages. First glue and cramp the two end frames. Set the cramped work to one side to allow the glue to harden. Then glue the two long rails to the end frames. Cramp, and again set the work aside for the glue to harden. Always check for accuracy of squareness before placing the work aside. Once modern glues have set, it is rarely possible to open up joints without breaking the wood from which they have been made. Clean off glue which has been squeezed out of the joints by cramping pressure. This can be done with the aid of a chisel or with pieces of clean wet rag.

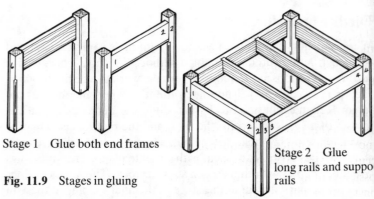

Stage 1   Glue both end frames

Stage 2   Glue long rails and support rails

Fig. 11.9   Stages in gluing

Secondary work and final cleaning-up

After gluing assemblies, there will nearly always be further work needing attention. The strips for holding the chipboard top to the

ame of the table will now have to be sawn to length, drilled and
en glued and screwed in position to the insides of the rails. The
erging of the mouldings along the bottoms of the rails into those
ong the legs must be formed with the aid of a carving gouge. The
orns on the legs must be sawn off and the upper edges of the frame
aned straight and flat. The outer surfaces of the frame must be
arefully cleaned up by planing and sanding. The chipboard top
ust be planed to fit on to its holding strips and inside the rails.
inally the chipboard top will have to be glued and screwed in
osition.

urface finish

ote that it is best if the tiles are cemented in place after a surface
nish has been applied. Always ensure that all surfaces to be
nished are quite clean and smooth. Most surface finishes will cause
urface defects to show up very clearly. The only answer to this
roblem is to ensure that all surface defects are removed. In the
xample of the tiled table, three coats of clear acid-catalysed
cquer are applied with a brush, allowing each coat to dry and
arden before applying the next. Note that the brush must be
oroughly cleaned in between coats, otherwise the lacquer will set
ard on its bristles and the brush will then be useless for other
urposes.

Finally, in this example, the tiles can be laid on the chipboard with
tile cement. The gaps between the tiles can then be filled with a tile
outing cement which has been coloured to match the colour of the
les.

milar procedures to those given in this chapter should be followed
hen making other pieces of woodwork in a workshop at a bench.
nce again, note the sequence followed: prepare all material
curately straight and square; mark out as much of the jointing as is
ossible; cut as much of the jointing as is possible; test whether the
onstruction will assemble; carry out any further work necessary;
ean all inside surfaces; glue and cramp and clean up ready for a
urface finish.

12

Wood Turning

The turning of wood has become a popular pastime for man people. This popularity has given rise to the development of a rang of machines, equipment and tools. The machine on which wood turned is called a 'lathe'. Three kinds of lathes are available: those designed specifically and solely for wood turning, those made to b attached to a power drill as an accessory and those which form or of the features of a multi-purpose machine. Power drill accessor lathes can perform a wide range of wood turning activities. The scope can however be limited by their size and by the amount of power generated by the electric motor of the power unit. The lathe of most of the multi-purpose machine lathes will allow longer wor to be turned than the power drill accessory type, and have th advantage that extra workshop space is not required for on machine specifically for wood turning. However, it is only on thos lathes designed solely for wood turning that a full range of heav work can be machined, such as the turning of large bowls and heav table legs, long work and similar operations. No matter which typ of lathe is considered, the basic principles on which they ar designed are the same. Fig. 12.1 shows a wood turning lathe de signed for heavy work in schools, colleges and in light industry, an illustrates the various parts of a typical wood turning lathe.

The wood turning lathe

The major purpose of a lathe is to enable wood to revolve in ord that the revolving wood can be shaped with tools. The headstoc contains a hollow spindle mounted in bearings. Each end of the spindle is threaded with a screw thread – a right-hand thread on the right-hand end and a left-hand thread on the other end. The right-hand end of the hole through the spindle is tapered to a standard Morse taper. Fittings such as faceplates or chucks can be screwed on either end of the spindle and a variety of 'centres' can be jammed into the tapered hole. Wood to be turned can be screwed on to faceplates, held in chucks, or held on a fork centre. The spindle is made to revolve by means of an electric motor in the headstock cabinet. The motor and spindle are connected by a V belt which runs over three or four step pulleys fitted to both the electric motor spindle and the lathe headstock spindle. The speeds at which the headstock spindle revolves are determined by changing the belt from one pair of pulley steps to another. Most lathes of the type shown in Fig. 12.1 can be adjusted in this way to produce speeds of from about 450 revolutions per minute (rpm) to about 2800 rpm, in either three or four stages. Large work such as wooden bowls of

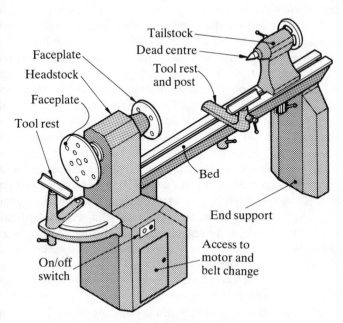

Fig. 12.1 The wood turning lathe

above, say, 150 mm (6 in) would be turned on the lowest speeds
Work of a small diameter, below, say, 30 mm (1¼ in), such as a set
of cricket stumps, would be turned on the higher speeds. By
variation of the spindle speed in relation to the diameter of the work
being turned, the actual speed at which wood is being cut remains
reasonably constant. Thus large diameter work uses slow spindle
speeds; small diameter work is carried out at fast spindle speeds.

The bed of a lathe carries a tailstock and a tool rest post. The
centre of the spindle and hence the centre of the dead centre above
the bed is an important measure of the size of a lathe. A lathe with
150 mm (6 in) centres would be capable of taking work mounted on
the right-hand end of the spindle no larger than a bare 300 mm
(12 in). This diameter is known as the 'swing' over the bed. The
lathe bed is either flat, cylindrical as shown in Fig. 12.4, a pair of
cylindrical rods or another form. No matter which type is used, the
bed must be straight, rigid and capable of carrying its headstock,
tailstock and tool rest post in such a manner that they can be slid
along the bed and firmly locked at any position along the bed. The
tailstock carries a hollow spindle, tapered at its left-hand end with a
Morse taper similar to that in the headstock spindle. 'Dead' centres
are jammed into this Morse taper hole. The term 'dead' refers to the
fact that a tailstock centre does not revolve. Headstock centres are
sometimes referred to as 'live' because they revolve and hence
move. The tailstock spindle can be made to slide within the tailstock
by means of a handle. This enables any length of work to be held
between headstock and tailstock. The tailstock spindle can also take
a drill chuck to enable work held on the headstock spindle to be
drilled. A Tee tool rest fitted in the tool post can be adjusted for
height and locked in its working position. Tools such as gouges and
chisels are held on the tool rest for working the wood being turned.
Lathes such as that illustrated carry an outrigger, on which a second
tool rest can be fitted. The outrigger tool rest allows large diameter
work to be fitted to the left-hand faceplate and turned. Special bowl
turning rests can be fitted in the tool post in place of the Tee rest to
allow large bowls to be made.

A lathe such as that shown would be powered by an electric motor
of between 0.75 and 1.25 horsepower. It would be controlled by a
press button on/off switch, which switches off automatically if mains
power is switched off. Work of up to 1 m (39 in) in length could be

eld between its centres. The two pedestals on which the lathe is
ounted would be made of very strong and rigid pressed steel.
owever all wood turning lathes are similar in that they possess
eadstocks and tailstocks, fitted to a bed on to which a tool rest can
e locked. Their headstock spindles are connected to a power
ource of some kind. On the smaller lathes, such as those run from a
ower drill, no facility for turning large diameters, such as on the
ft-hand faceplate shown in Fig. 12.1, would be available.

ypes of centres and chucks

g. 12.2 shows a small selection of the variety of fittings which can
e screwed to the threads of a lathe spindle or held in the Morse
pers of the spindles. Fork centres can be forced into one end of the
ood to be turned, the other end of the wood being held by a dead
entre. The fork centre held in the Morse taper of the headstock
indle forces the wood to rotate when the electric motor is switched
1. The wood is held in position at its other end, rotating on the
ead centre. A screw chuck is designed for holding small items on to
e lathe spindle while they are turned. The wood is simply screwed
1 to the wood screw of the chuck, which in turn is screwed on the
ose of the headstock spindle. Other forms of chuck include drill
ucks, collet chucks for holding thin diameter metal, cup chucks
to which wood can be forced, coil chucks in which wood is held by
rings, three-jaw chucks and faceplates on to which wood can be
rewed with wood screws. Other forms of 'chucking' devices are
so available. The most frequently used are faceplates for faceplate
rning and fork centres with dead centres for 'between centres'
rning.

rk
tre

Dead
centres

Screw
chuck

Fig. 12.2 Types of centres and a chuck

Wood turning tools

Three types of turning tool are mainly used. These are gouge
chisels and scrapers. All rough turning to size and rough shaping
carried out with turning gouges. Turning gouges are sturdie
heavier and larger than bench or carving gouges. They need to b
stronger because of the great strains involved on them when wood
turned. Turning gouges are also sharpened in a different manner t
bench and carving gouges. They are sharpened so that the end of th
tool is rounded instead of being straight and square with the side a
in other gouges. The angles of sharpening; 25° for grinding and 3(
for honing; are however the same. Note the long handles, made to
shape only found on turning tools, which are made from beech c
ash. The overall length of handle and blade averages about 600 m
(24 in). Turning gouges can be purchased with blades of 6 mn
13 mm, 19 mm and 25 mm (¼ in, ½ in, ¾ in and 1 in) width
While smaller and larger sizes are of value for shaping concav
curves when turning, most turning for which gouges are designe
can be carried out with a 19 mm (¾ in) width gouge. Turnin
chisels, of the same length overall as the gouges, are alway
sharpened as shown, on both sides of the blade with the cutting edg
at about 60° to the blade edges. This 'skew' sharpening allows th
chisel to cut without its corners digging into the wood as it turn
Despite the fact that the sharpening angles are on both sides, the
should be retained at 25° and 30° for grinding and honing. Widths c
chisel blade of 13 mm, 19 mm, 25 mm and 35 mm (½ in, ¾ in

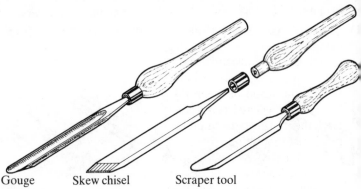

Gouge   Skew chisel   Scraper tool

Fig. 12.3   Hand tools for turning

in, 1⅜ in) are made, but most work can be carried out with a
25 mm chisel. Scraper chisels do not cut, but scrape. Because of this
they are sharpened at the very steep angle of 75° to 80°. The one
shown in Fig. 12.3 has a rounded end, but flat-ended, V-ended,
hollow-ended scrapers can also be purchased, or made. A common
practice among experienced turners is to make their own scraper
chisels from old worn-out or discarded files. These are shaped on a
grinding wheel, the file cuts are removed by grinding and the shaped
ends then honed on an oilstone.

Fig. 12.4 shows the three types of turning tool in use. Gouges and
chisels are positioned in such a manner that they will cut and
produce shavings. This means that they should be held almost
tangentially to the wood as it is turned and the angle of the tool
adjusted until a cutting action takes place. Scraper tools however
are always positioned so that the upper surface of their blades are at
90° to the work being shaped. Despite the fact that scraper tools do
not cut waste from the work, but scrape it away, some woods such as
box, rosewood and other very hard woods, can be worked to a very
good smooth surface with scraper tools. Softwoods and hardwoods
such as oak or ash, which tend to scrape badly, with resulting rough
surfaces, are best worked with turning chisels.

Methods of wood turning

As an example of how work is turned, Fig. 12.5 shows stages in the
making of a simple reading lamp stand. Drawings 1 to 3 show how
the stand is made. Drawings 4 to 7 show how the base is made.

1 Plane the corners of a piece of square wood to a roughly
   octagonal (8-sided) section. Fit a fork centre in the headstock
   spindle and a dead centre in the tailstock. Fit the wood between
   the centres and, after locking the tailstock on the lathe bed,
   tighten the wood between the centres. A little grease on the
   dead centre will assist easy running of the wood.
2 Lock the tool post in a suitable position on the lathe bed. Adjust
   the T rest to a suitable height. Turn to the shape required with
   gouge and chisel. Sand to a smooth surface with sandpaper.
3 Place a drill chuck in the headstock spindle. With the aid of the
   tailstock adjusting handle, drive the turned work on to the drill,
   working from each end to bore the hole right through.

4   Screw a faceplate on to a piece of wood cut roughly circular in shape. Saw the lamp base roughly circular in shape. Glue the two pieces of wood to each other with a disc of stout paper between.

5   With gouge and chisel shape the outer part of the base. With a flat scraper chisel work a recess in the base. Split the paper between the two pieces of wood, thus releasing the turned part.

6   Shape the wood remaining on the faceplate to a boss which will fit precisely into the recess in the lamp base. Again glue the base to the wood on the faceplate with paper between.

7   Complete the shaping of the base. Scraper tools will probably be required for the curves and to obtain the hole into which the peg at the bottom of the upright part should tightly fit. Sand to a smooth surface. Split the paper to release the turned base. Glue the upright into the base. Felt or baize can be glued into the recess at the base of the completed stand.

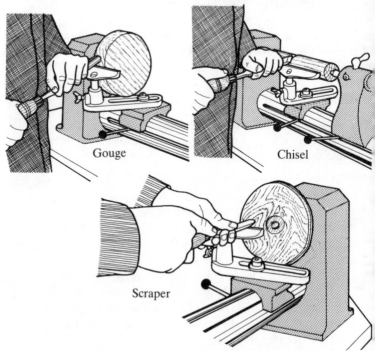

Fig. 12.4   Methods of using turning tools

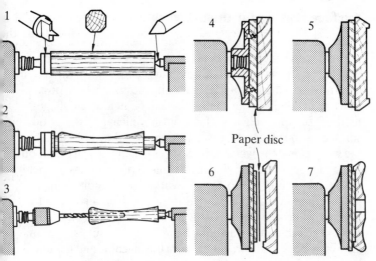

Fig. 12.5 Stages in turning a reading lamp

Fig. 12.6 shows how a turning gouge and a turning chisel would be employed to form the shape of the vertical part of the reading lamp stand. The order of operations is indicated by the numbers 1 to 4 in the illustration. First, the outline of the long curve along the piece would be turned roughly to shape with the gouge. Second, the turning chisel would be employed to cut the curve to its exact final shape. Third, the shoulder of the tenon plug would be cut with the tip of the chisel. Finally, the tenon would be reduced to its finished diameter with the turning chisel.

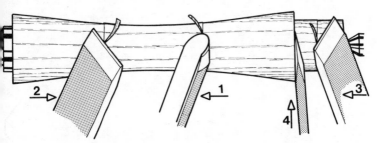

Fig. 12.6 Cutting actions of turning gouge and chisel

Surface finishes for turned work

As good a surface finish as possible should always be obtained b
sanding with sandpapers before releasing work from a lathe. Wit
work between centres, it is always advisable to finish the sanding b
carefully working the sandpaper along the grain where possible. N
block is needed, as the sandpaper can be held in the fingers. On
method of applying a surface finish which gives a good, clea
surface, is to rub carnuba wax into the wood by holding a block o
the wax against the wood as it revolves. Then burnish the wood wit
clean rag, or even clean shavings, whilst it revolves. Any other woo
finish can be applied to turned work, for example french polish
polyurethane or acid catalysed lacquers. It is advisable to appl
finishes while the work is still held in chucks on the lathe. Thi
avoids the difficulty of actually handling the turnings. This may no
always be possible however because the machine and its chucks ma
be needed for other work.

Woods for turning

A skilled and practised wood turner will be able to produce smoot
clean turnery in practically any wood. Some excellent woods whic
produce good turned work are beech, birch, box, lime, rosewood
sycamore and yew. With care, and providing sufficient skill wit
turning chisels has been developed, you will be able to produc
smooth turned surfaces in other woods. It is in the manipulation o
sharp skew turning chisels that such surfaces can be obtained.

13

Some Household Woodwork

Fitting shelves into an alcove

Fitting shelves is probably one of the most common jobs around the house. Shelves can be made from various materials. Pine or hardwood boards are very suitable and, if well finished, provide attractive features in a room. Such boards are strong; 25 mm (1 in) thick wooden boards will provide adequate support for heavy loads in lengths up to 1 m (39 in) long. Chipboard, either plain or veneered, makes good shelving, but should be supported underneath by strengthening strips screwed along the length of each shelf from underneath (see Fig. 13.1). Thinner boards should be supported in the same way. Plywood or hardboard will provide good shelving given support from a frame (see Fig. 13.1).

The most simple form of shelving consists of boards fitted on wall bearers in an alcove. Bearers can be screwed to a wall via wall plugs in holes bored in the wall with masonry drills. The bearers need be no larger than about 30 mm by 15 mm (1¼ in by ⅝ in). If you wish to hide the screw heads, glue a strip of veneer over the bearer. All shelves must be fitted so that their surfaces are horizontal and it is best to check their surfaces with a spirit level before finally fixing them in position. The last 4 drawings in Fig. 13.1 show the method of fitting a nest of shelves into an alcove. The sequence is as follows:

1   Cut a board to length to rest on the skirting boards to act as a bottom shelf. A plinth can be fitted to the underside of this shelf as shown in drawing 7 in Fig. 13.1.

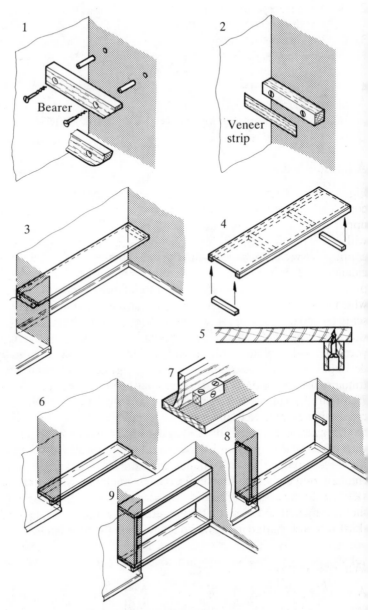

Fig. 13.1 Fitting shelves into alcoves

2   Screw bearers to the insides of the vertical sides making up the
    sides of the bookshelf unit. Place these sides in position.
3   Cut the middle shelf exactly to length to fit on the bearers and in
    between the vertical sides. This shelf should fit tightly enough to
    hold the sides firmly against the walls.
4   Now fit the top shelf. If this is a snug fit between the walls of the
    alcove, there is no real need to secure it to the ends of the vertical
    sides, as the weight of books on the top shelf should hold it quite
    securely in its position.

A framed wardrobe

Fig. 13.2 gives details of a wardrobe which could be fitted into the
corner of a bedroom. This wardrobe consists of three cupboards: an
upper cupboard for hats and spare clothing, a central cupboard,
with a clothes hanging rail, for coats, dresses and suits, and a lower
cupboard which could be used to store such items as a vacuum
cleaner. The wardrobe consists of a framework made from lengths
of planed softwood 35 mm (1⅜ in) wide and 25 mm (1 in) thick,
which is screwed on to strips of 15 mm (⅝ in) square material,
screwed to the walls, ceiling and floor via wall plugs. The sizes of the
wardrobe and its parts will depend upon the size of the room and
your personal requirements, but a good depth of 610 mm (24 in) is
desirable to give adequate space for hanging clothes. The
framework consists of two parts, which are nailed to each other with
75 mm (3 in) long nails. Each part is jointed with corner, Tee and
cross halvings, glued and pinned at each joint. When the framework
has been made, it can be screwed to the wall bearers and then clad
with hardboard or plywood. Doors made from hardboard or ply-
wood-clad halving jointed frames are hung on the frame using
cranked hinges. Door frames could be made from lengths of
softwood 25 mm (1 in) wide and 15 mm (⅝ in) thick. The cladding
should be glued and pinned. To complete the wardrobe a length of
skirting board is fitted along its side, and it can then be painted.

Wardrobe from chipboard

A wardrobe of similar design could be made from wood or plastic
veneered chipboard. Details of its construction are shown in

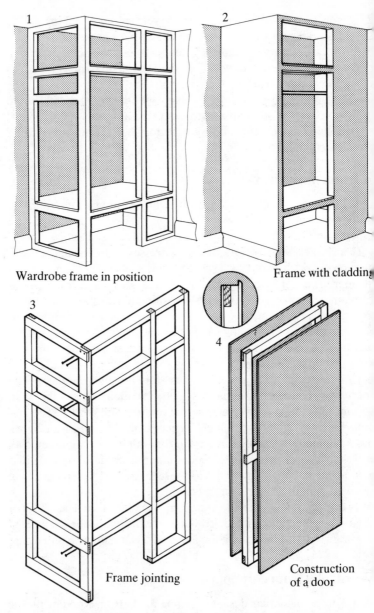

1 Wardrobe frame in position

2 Frame with cladding

3 Frame jointing

4 Construction of a door

Fig. 13.2 Fitting a wardrobe into a corner of a bedroom

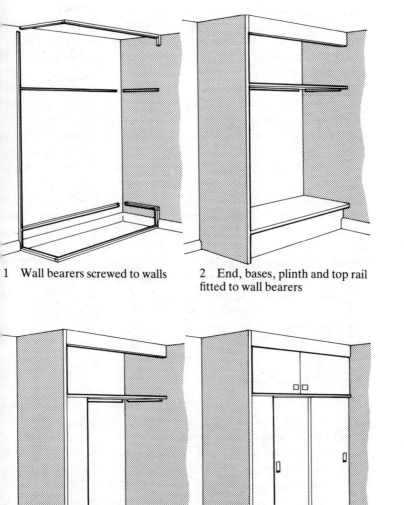

1 Wall bearers screwed to walls

2 End, bases, plinth and top rail fitted to wall bearers

3 Front piece fitted

4 Doors fitted

Fig. 13.3 Fitting a wardrobe made from veneered chipboard

Fig. 13.3. When using veneered chipboard, some constructional precautions need to be observed. Chipboard is liable to bend and even break when used in unsupported large areas. The sheets thus need to be supported along their length and across their width. The support for the large end of the wardrobe shown is provided by the two cupboard base boards across its width and by the vertical wall batten and chipboard front along its length. The top front rail and plinth also strengthen the end. Begin by screwing wall bearers to the walls. Join the plinth rail to the chipboard base of the wardrobe and fit and screw this assembly to the top of the base wall bearers. The baseboard for the upper cupboard is also screwed down on to its supporting wall bearers. The wardrobe end can now be fitted into place against the bearers screwed to wall, ceiling and floor. Now fit the top rail, also screwed (from the rear) to a ceiling bearer and short bearers on the end and on the wall. A front panel can now be fitted using nylon joint blocks between it, the end and the two base boards. The larger wardrobe doors run on purpose-made sliding door fittings which can be purchased for the purpose. The two upper cupboard doors are hung on hinges. The right-hand door hinges can either be screwed into wall plugs in the wall or onto a strip of wood which is itself screwed to the wall.

Hanging a room door

Whether the door which is to be hung is a flush door or a panelled door, the process of hanging will be the same. After planing the edges of the door so that it is a good fit in its doorway, taking care to make an allowance for any necessary coats of paint, place the door in position mounted on wedges. By slightly withdrawing or tapping in the wedges, which lowers or raises the door slightly, the exact position for the door can be found. When satisfied with its position, place the hinges in position over the edge of the door and mark their lengths on to both the door and on the side of the doorway with the aid of a pencil. Now mark out recesses on both the door edge and on the doorway edge. After cutting the recesses, the hinges can be screwed in position on the door, and then it can be hung by screwing through the hinge holes into the recesses in the doorway. Fig. 13.4 illustrates the processes involved in hanging a door.

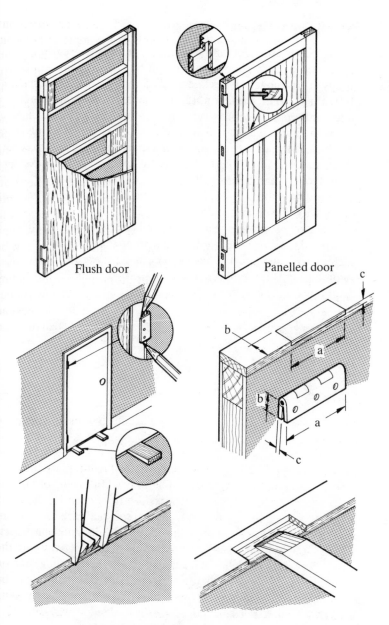

Flush door

Panelled door

Fig. 13.4 Hanging a room door

Simple upholstery

Using polyurethane foam slabs when upholstering seats makes the operation a fairly simple one. Foam block is readily available in shops in a range of thicknesses: 25 mm (1 in), 50 mm (2 in), 100 mm (4 in) are common. It is advisable to insist on fire-resistant foam and on high-density types for seating. Foam block on sale is often medium density which is somewhat soft for seating. Foam block can be readily cut to size with a sharp knife, or can be sawn or shaped with a hot wire cutter, if one is available. Foam blocks can be mounted on hardboard, plywood or chipboard, but ventilation holes must be bored through such seat boards to allow for the escape of air when the seat is sat upon.

To make a complete seat, foam can be fixed to a seat frame. If a square-edged seat is required, strap foam to the seat with tape which is glued with an impact adhesive to both the foam and the frame. If rounded edges are required, either of the two methods shown in the diagrams can be employed.

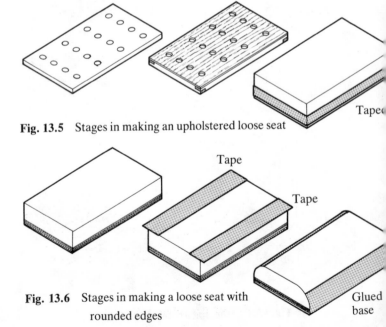

Fig. 13.5   Stages in making an upholstered loose seat

Fig. 13.6   Stages in making a loose seat with
rounded edges

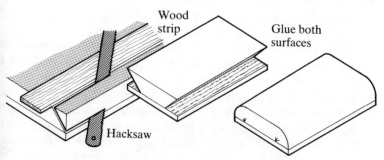

Fig. 13.7 Another method of forming rounded edges

A loose seat cushion from foam

First cut the foam slab to size. The slab must be cut slightly larger than required for the finished seat, otherwise the seat will not look trimly rectangular. An allowance of about 2 mm every 100 mm

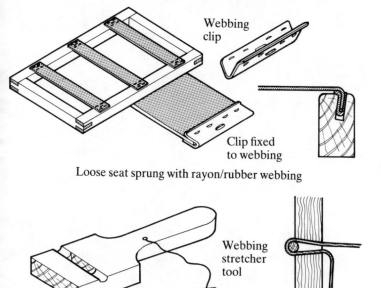

Fig. 13.8 Details of a sprung loose seat

(¼ in per ft) added in all directions is needed. If the envelope for a loose seat is to be made from a vinyl material, either add eyelets in the lower part of the cover or make the bottom of the cover from a cotton material which will allow air to escape as the seat is compressed when sat upon.

If you wish to make a sprung seat, rayon and rubber webbing will provide an excellent support. This form of webbing can either be tacked directly on to a frame support or can be fitted to the frame with webbing clips which are clipped into purpose made grooves cut in the frame. If the webbing is tacked (or stapled) to its seating frame, a webbing stretcher tool such as the one shown in Fig. 13.8 will be of value. When fitting foam on this form of webbing, cover the webbing with hessian or some other form of coarsely woven cloth to prevent the foam becoming damaged by the frame and the webbing. The webbing clips are forced on to the webbing with the aid of a bench vice.

Appendix A

Metric and Imperial Dimensions

Throughout this book both metric and imperial dimensions have been quoted. The normal practice in woodwork is to give metric dimensions in millimetres or occasionally, when long sizes are required, dimensions can be quoted in metres and millimetres, or in metres as decimals. Thus dimensions such as:

6 mm	26 mm	190 mm	1300 mm	2790 mm
1 m 500 m		3 m 100 m	2.450 m	7.419 m

will be seen on drawings showing designs in wood. When drawings are dimensioned in imperial units, sizes are quoted in inches and in fractions of an inch. The unit of a foot is also common for larger dimensions. Thus dimensions such as the following will be seen on drawings for woodwork designs when imperial units are used:

¼″	1″	7³⁄₁₆″	18″	23¼″
1′0¼″		2′3″	4′7½″	3′9⅞″

Note that a common practice used by woodworkers is to give dimensions up to 24 inches in inch units and from 24 inches in feet and inches. This practice derives from the traditional types of common 24-inch long rules.

Conversion from metric to imperial

One inch equals 25.4 millimetres. For most practical purposes, when working in wood, it is convenient to convert each inch to 25 millimetres. Thus 1 in = 25 mm; 2 in = 50 mm; 3 in = 75 mm; 4 in = 100 mm, is convenient for most dimensions up to about 12 inches.

For greater accuracy, a table such as the following should be used, in which 1 inch = 25.4 millimetres is the conversion ratio.

inches		mm	inches		mm	inches		mm	inches		mm
⅛	=	3.175	5	=	127	18	=	457.2	31	=	787.4
3/16	=	4.7625	6	=	152.4	19	=	482.6	32	=	812.8
¼	=	6.35	7	=	177.8	20	=	508	33	=	838.2
5/16	=	7.9375	8	=	203.2	21	=	533.4	34	=	863.6
⅜	=	9.525	9	=	228.6	22	=	558.8	35	=	889
½	=	12.7	10	=	254	23	=	584.2	36	=	914.4
⅝	=	15.875	11	=	279.4	24	=	609.6	37	=	939.8
¾	=	19.05	12	=	304.8	25	=	635	38	=	965.2
⅞	=	22.225	13	=	330.2	26	=	660.4	39	=	990.6
1	=	25.4	14	=	355.6	27	=	685.8	40	=	1016
2	=	50.8	15	=	381	28	=	711.2			
3	=	76.2	16	=	406.4	29	=	736.6			
4	=	101.6	17	=	431.8	30	=	762			

Appendix B

Woods

Softwoods

Cedar   Western red cedar. Red brown. Light in weight. Scented. Resists rotting without added finish. All outdoor work.

Douglas fir   British Columbian pine. Light red brown. Very distinct grain. Almost knot-free. Heavy constructional work. Laminated arches. Joinery.

Larch   Resinous. Straight grained. Knot free. Tough and durable. Boat building. Exterior work in contact with ground.

Parana pine   Brazilian. Straight grained. Knot-free. Hard and heavy for a softwood. Coach building, joinery, door frames. Not durable.

Pitch pine   Hard and heavy. Distinct grain. Dark yellow brown. Very durable. Heavy constructional work – lorry and rail wagons. Heavy flooring.

Redwood   Scots pine. The common building timber. Very wide use. Joinery, carpentry, 'Pine' furniture, flooring, roofing etc.

Spruce   Several types. Canadian spruce – strong and flexible for its weight. Canoe frames. Canoe paddles. Glider frames. Non-durable, so no good for outdoor work. White spruce, or whitewood, is used for general joinery. Not so flexible as Canadian (Sitka) spruce.

Yellow pine   Easily worked. Straight grained. Medium weight. Good quality joinery. Pattern making for moulding industry.

Yew   Irregular, decorative grain. Hard and heavy. A most prized decorative furniture wood. Turned work.

Hardwoods

The following lists only a few of the more frequently used hardwoods from the thousands of different species in commercial use.

Afrormosia   West Africa. Yellow brown. Fairly straight-grained. Heavy and tough. Furniture. Railway carriage building. Some shipbuilding.

Agba   Congo. Light uniform brown. Medium weight. Easy working. Furniture. Joinery. Not suitable for contact with food because of resinous odour.

Apple   Europe. Hard to work. Turnery.

Ash   Europe. Light brown. Distinct grain. Tough and flexible. Bends extremely well. Gymnastic apparatus. Hammer and pick handles. Billiard cues.

Balsa   Ecuador. Light brown. Very light in weight. Rapid growth. An excellent model making timber. Aircraft models.

Beech   Europe. Straight-grained. White to pale brown. Pink brown when steamed. Tools. Bench tops. Turnery. Plywood.

Birch   Europe. Straight-grained. Light colour. Fine texture. Plywood. Turning.

Boxwood   Europe and Middle East. Yellow. Very fine grain. Turnery. Rulers. Mallet heads. Chessmen.

Cherry   Europe. Fine, even texture. Pale pink brown. High class cabinet and furniture work. Turnery.

Chestnut   Europe. Pale brown with clear and distinct grain. Easy working. Furniture making. Fence palings.

Ebony   India. Very heavy, fine, even textured black wood. Fancy work. Instrument finger boards. Inlaying.

Elm   Europe. Dull brown with distinct grain. Furniture. Coffin making. Boat building.

Greenheart   Gyana. Hard, even textured, heavy. Olive green. Fishing rods. Heavy constructional work.

Holly   Europe. Green white or grey. Hard, even textured. Inlays.

Iroko   West and Central Africa. Medium weight. Dark brown. Interlocking grain. Exterior and interior joinery. Vehicle and wagon building.

Jelotung   Malaya. Produces rubber. White or straw colour. Light weight. Soft and easy to work. Model and pattern making.

Lignum Vitae   South America. Hardest and heaviest timber known. Dark greenish-brown. Mallet heads. Turnery. 'Woods' for bowling.

Lime   Europe. Soft, yet compact. Excellent for carving.

Mahogany   Honduras. Light red-brown. Straight grain. Easy working. High class furniture.

Oak   Europe. Yellow-brown. Distinct ray markings. Furniture. Joinery. Church fittings.

Obeche   Nigeria. White to pale straw colour. Straight-grained. Easy working. Linings in furniture.

Ramin   Malaya. Pale straw. Straight-grained. Easy working. Furniture. Joinery. Turnery generally.

Rosewood   India. Dark purple-brown. Uniform grain. High class furniture and cabinet making.

Sycamore   Europe. Fine texture. White or yellow-white. Good lustre. Turning. Furniture making. Violin backs.

Teak   Burma. Straight-grained. Brown. A valuable timber. Large variety of uses. High quality window and door frames. Furniture making.

Utile   West Africa. Reddish to purple-brown. Usually even texture. Works well. Cabinet making. Lorry frames.

Walnut   Europe. Grey-brown with very variable grain markings. Veneered work. Rifle butts. Furniture of high class.

Index